East-West Relations
in Europe

Westview Replica Editions

The concept of Westview Replica Editions is a response to the continuing crisis in academic and informational publishing. Library budgets for books have been severely curtailed. Ever larger portions of general library budgets are being diverted from the purchase of books and used for data banks, computers, micromedia, and other methods of information retrieval. Interlibrary loan structures further reduce the edition sizes required to satisfy the needs of the scholarly community. Economic pressures on the university presses and the few private scholarly publishing companies have severely limited the capacity of the industry to properly serve the academic and research communities. As a result, many manuscripts dealing with important subjects, often representing the highest level of scholarship, are no longer economically viable publishing projects--or, if accepted for publication, are typically subject to lead times ranging from one to three years.

Westview Replica Editions are our practical solution to the problem. We accept a manuscript in camera-ready form, typed according to our specifications, and move it immediately into the production process. As always, the selection criteria include the importance of the subject, the work's contribution to scholarship, and its insight, originality of thought, and excellence of exposition. The responsibility for editing and proofreading lies with the author or sponsoring institution. We prepare chapter headings and display pages, file for copyright, and obtain Library of Congress Cataloging in Publication Data. A detailed manual contains simple instructions for preparing the final typescript, and our editorial staff is always available to answer questions.

The end result is a book printed on acid-free paper and bound in sturdy library-quality soft covers. We manufacture these books ourselves using equipment that does not require a lengthy make-ready process and that allows us to publish first editions of 300 to 600 copies and to reprint even smaller quantities as needed. Thus, we can produce Replica Editions quickly and can keep even very specialized books in print as long as there is a demand for them.

About the Book and Author

East-West Relations in Europe:
Observations and Advice from the Sidelines, 1971-1982
Paul E. Zinner

As scholar, researcher, and commentator, Dr. Paul E. Zinner
has spent much of the last six years in Europe studying the development of East-West relations, observing negotiations on arms
reduction, and conducting interviews with foreign policy and
national security experts from key countries. This book
brings together eleven of his essays--nearly all previously
unpublished--that emphasize developments since 1977. The essays
cover a broad range of topics, among them the status and prospects of the Vienna troops reduction talks; the political and
military implications of NATO's "double track" decision concerning modernization of intermediate-range nuclear forces in
Europe; the impact of the crises in Afghanistan and Poland on the
Western alliance; and the foreign policy options available to the
Reagan administration. Also included are assessments of current
trends in the NATO alliance and a cautious projection of the
political climate in Western Europe by the end of the 1980s.
Updated throughout with introductory and commentary notes, the
essays provide insight into the dominant themes in the interaction between the NATO and Warsaw Pact powers.

Since 1961, Dr. Zinner has taught at the University of California at Davis where he is currently professor of political
science. For many years he was a frequent commentator on *World
Press,* a weekly PBS television program.

East-West Relations in Europe

Observations and Advice from the Sidelines, 1971–1982

Paul E. Zinner

Westview Press / Boulder, Colorado

A Westview Replica Edition

Copyright©1984 by Westview Press, Inc.

Published in 1984 in the United States of America by
   Westview Press, Inc.
   5500 Central Avenue
   Boulder, Colorado 80301
   Frederick A. Praeger, President and Publisher

Library of Congress Cataloging in Publication Data
Zinner, Paul E.
   East-West relations in Europe.
   (A Westview replica edition)
   1. Europe--Foreign relations--1945-   --Addresses, essays, lectures.
2. Europe--Defenses--History--20th century--Addresses, essays, lectures.
3. Poland--Politics and government--1980-   --Addresses, essays, lectures.
4. North Atlantic Treaty Organization--Addresses, essays, lectures.
I. Title.
D1058.Z54   1983   327.4   83-14544
ISBN 0-86531-988-X

Printed and bound in the United States of America

10 9 8 7 6 5 4 3 2

Dedicated to
GEORGE ZINNER
and
GEORGE PAUL ROBERT ZINNER

Contents

Acknowledgments. xi
Introduction xiii

1 ON THE BRINK OF DETENTE   1

Soviet Foreign Policy in Transition
   (February 1971)   3

2 PROBLEMS AND PROSPECTS OF TROOP REDUCTIONS
   IN CENTRAL EUROPE 27

Observations about the Vienna Negotiations
   on Mutual and Balanced Force Reductions
   (December 1977) 28

3 BENEFICIARY OF DETENTE. 57

The Federal Republic of Germany on the
   Threshold of the 1980s (October 1979).   58

4 RESURGENT CONFRONTATION BETWEEN
   EAST AND WEST 73

United States Response to the Threat of the
   Soviet SS-20 (October 1979).   75
Effects of the Crises in Afghanistan and
   Poland on Relations between the United States
   and Western Europe (November 1980)   78
Eastern Europe--Still Unresolved
   (December 1980)   84
Reagan's Foreign Policy Options
   (January 1981).   89
Military and Political Implications of NATO's
   "Double Track" Decision on Modernizing
   Long-Range Theater Nuclear Forces
   (October 1981).   92
The Fate of Poland: Dilemma for the West
   (February 1982) 105

5 A LOOK INTO THE 1980s 119

   NATO: Trends and Alternatives
      (July 1982) 121

   Western Europe between the Superpowers
      (September 1982). 138

Acknowledgments

Writing acknowledgments is not without hazard. Either one is discriminating and runs the risk of offending individuals who feel slighted at being left out, or one is not discriminating, in which case the list of credits becomes diluted and devoid of meaning.

With apologies to those who might take umbrage at not having their assistance acknowledged, I wish to give heartfelt thanks to my wife Joan for her sustained encouragement and practical help, and to my daughter Vickie and my son John for their invaluable support.

I should like to express profound gratitude to Dierk Clausen, Horst Hartwich, Helmut Wagner, Hannelore Horn, Hans-Adolf Jacobsen, and Hansjürgen and Renate von Kries. Without their initiative, the opportunities to return to Europe repeatedly and conduct research there simply would not have existed.

I am also beholden to Marvin Gustavson and Robert Squire.

Finally, I am grateful to Fred Praeger and his associates at Westview Press for reproducing and marketing this collection of essays.

Paul E. Zinner

Introduction

The hopes and expectations that attached to detente at its inception at the turn of the decade into the 1970s clearly have not been realized. They have given way to fears and apprehensions about an uncertain future, fraught with the danger of nuclear devastation. This change in attitude cannot be ascribed solely to disenchantment on the part of many people in the West with the self-delusions to which they had fallen prey. Nor is it enough to lay the blame on the single-minded buildup of Soviet military power, which increasing numbers of people, particularly in the United States, have come to regard as evidence of an unrelenting drive by the Soviet Union to achieve a hegemonic position in Europe, if not on a global scale. Although it is a plausible assumption that the Soviet Union strives for a dominant position in Europe, not everyone, especially in Europe, holds this viewpoint. The vicissitudes that have overtaken East-West relations in Europe cannot be satisfactorily explained by reference to a single factor.

There is no doubt that in the initial stages of detente the promise of this attempt to restructure East-West relations was unwarrantedly exalted. By the same token, in a later period the failure of detente to fulfill euphoric expectations was judged with undue harshness.

Given the fundamental incompatibilities between the alliance systems, it is not astonishing that the balance sheet of detente should be negative. The ties that bind the two alliance systems are artificial and too flimsy to provide the foundations for a stable and lasting security partnership between them, provided that such a relationship is desirable. If anything, detente has tended to reveal in bold relief precisely how irreconcilable are some of the differences between East and West, how narrow are the limits of tolerance within which acceptable accommodations can be reached. A readiness to compromise would have to be predicated on the existence of at least a modicum of mutual confidence, despite deeply entrenched reciprocal suspicions. The essential ingredient, trust, has been conspicuously missing from the equation.

Detente opened new opportunities to both sides and confronted both with new challenges. Surprises and disappointments have been shared by them in roughly equal proportions. Both sides have had to adapt to new ways of interacting and, at least on a limited scale, to accommodate their adversaries who took on the guise of partners. Interaction has inevitably meant interpenetration. It has induced fluidity, increased unpredictability, and undermined the ability of the superpowers to control their allies and thus their political environment. A relaxation of the cramped posture of the antagonistic sides (which is one descriptive way of characterizing detente) has brought in its wake a loosening of relations within each alliance, more so in the West, perhaps, but not unappreciably in the East. We note the centrifugal tendencies in the Western alliance and, indeed, they have been pronounced; but there has been nothing comparable in the West to the cataclysmic events that have overtaken Poland and rocked the Eastern bloc to its foundations.

The experiences of the past decade or so teach both hard and valuable lessons. But how much have the participants learned? And how much of what they have learned causes them to continue probing the prospect of further cooperative interaction, instead of repudiating similar experimentation as too dangerous to their security?

A thorough analysis of detente in all its dimensions and with all its ramifications remains to be written. This modest volume makes no pretense at being a substitute for such a study. It comprises eleven short essays, written at irregular intervals over a period of eleven years and organized, for want of a more rational scheme, in five chronologically arranged chapters. Except for the first essay (the only one previously published), all the essays are by-products of extensive field research I have conducted in Europe since 1977. The rationale for presenting this collection of essays in a single tome at this time is twofold: they seem timely and pertinent.

Nine of the essays deal with major discrete aspects of East-West relations in Europe; two probe future trends in NATO and among Western European countries. The subjects dealt with include: constants and variables in Soviet foreign policy; efforts to negotiate an agreement on troop reductions in Central Europe; perceptions that prevailed in the Federal Republic of Germany in the late 1970s about the country's security problems; the reasons for and the consequences of the NATO "double track" decision on long-range theater nuclear force modernization; the impact of international crises on the cohesiveness of the Western alliance in the early 1980s; and the domestic and international repercussions attendant upon the Polish events at the beginning of the current decade.

Although I have made no deliberate attempt to integrate systematically the material contained in the individual essays nor to develop coherent theoretical postulates, the reader should not find it difficult to discern dominant themes and prominent evolutionary patterns: the growth of a perceptual gap between the United States and its West European allies, which leads to a gradual loosening of the bonds in the Atlantic partnership; the concomitant rise in Europe of a felt community of interests especially among the smaller Western and Eastern powers, including neutral and non-aligned countries; the corollary disposition of some countries in Western Europe to respond positively to the exertions of the Soviet Union to identify itself with this community of European interests; the affirmation of the pivotal place that the Federal Republic of Germany has in European affairs; the influence that the unique dependence and vulnerability of the Federal Republic has on its susceptibility to outside manipulation; the surfacing of the "German question" in the guise of a special relationship between the two German states, which becomes ever more pronounced and forms a crucial subset in the broader framework of East-West relations; the resurgence of superpower hostility in a bilateral and global context, which tends to encroach on regional multilateral processes of interaction; and the persistence in the Soviet Union of structural impediments to "genuine detente" (in our Western sense of the term).

I will feel richly rewarded if the contents of these essays shed light on and create greater awareness about the complex nature of East-West relations in Europe, and if they stimulate interest in the reader to become still better informed about the problems discussed here. I could not hope for more than that the notes I have jotted down on the margin of time should help to impart--especially to young readers--perspectives on international issues with which they soon will have to cope, and thus contribute to their preparation for assuming responsibilities from which they can escape only at their own peril.

Paul E. Zinner
September 1983

1
On the Brink of Detente

      This appraisal of Soviet foreign policy in transi-
tion was first delivered as a lecture at the National
War College in Washington, D.C., in the fall of 1970.
Subsequently, it appeared as an article in the spring
1971 issue of the National War College _Forum_. The
nature of the occasion called for a review or tour
d'horizon of Soviet policies in major geographic areas,
if not around the world. My aim was to outline an
analytic framework in which Soviet foreign policy might
be usefully evaluated and to project certain policy
trends that might be anticipated. Straws of change in
the orientation of American and Soviet foreign policies
were in the wind. Yet in specific detail, the Soviet-
American relationship bristled with hostility.
      It is clear from what I wrote that I did not
expect detente to be consummated as soon as May 1972,
at which time a summit meeting between President
Richard Nixon and Secretary General Leonid I. Brezhnev
took place in Moscow. Obviously, I was not privy to
closely guarded preparatory negotiations. Foreign
Minister Andrei A. Gromyko's extraordinary speech in
July 1969 (from which I quote at some length) clearly
signaled that the general line of Soviet foreign policy
was about to change. Gromyko's son Anatoly, who
visited me in California in 1970, cautiously and without giving away any secrets intimated that a peace
offensive would be unveiled at the forthcoming Twenty-
fourth Congress of the Communist party of the Soviet
Union (CPSU). The congress, which convened in March
1971 when my analysis was already typeset, indeed inau-
gurated a comprehensive "peace program" under the aegis
of detente. The term itself was significant. It appeared to have been deliberately selected to differen-
tiate the new policy from the more familiar policy of
"peaceful coexistence" dating back to Lenin, toward
which the West, after repeated disappointments, had
developed a skeptical, not to say jaundiced, attitude.

1

From the perspective of 1983, it is evident that events did not always correspond to my expectations and that my judgment was faulty in certain particulars. For example, I did not anticipate that Soviet influence in the Middle East would decline precipitously after Anwar Sadat emerged as the successor to the deceased Egyptian President Gamal Abdel Nasser. Nor did I foresee that Soviet policy in South America would be severely set back in 1973 by the overthrow of the Allende regime in Chile. I was wrong in suggesting that a generational change in the Soviet Union might be in the offing; nothing of the sort occurred. Instead, Leonid Brezhnev systematically eliminated his younger rivals and replaced them in high government and party office by his aging contemporaries. The survival and dominance of this generation, even after Brezhnev's death in November 1982, is one of the more remarkable phenomena in the evolution of the Soviet political system.

I believe that I was more nearly correct in estimating the general thrust of Soviet foreign policy; the constancy of the basic determinants of the Soviet worldview; the recurring obstacles in the way of a permanent improvement in Soviet-American relations; and, perhaps especially, the growing importance of military power and power of the military in shaping the foreign policies of the superpowers.

In the light of subsequent developments, my critical attitude toward the initial stages of the Ostpolitik introduced by the West German Social Democratic leadership (which had recently been elected to govern the Federal Republic in coalition with the liberal Free Democratic party) may seem excessively harsh. Early misgivings shared by Henry Kissinger (as recorded by the former secretary of state in his memoirs) and by West German conservatives (who had just been ousted from office and, in addition to genuine convictions, also had political motives for opposing a drastic reorientation of foreign policy) dissipated rather quickly. By mid-1972, the Eastern treaties and agreements, regulating relations with the Soviet Union, the German Democratic Republic, and the People's Republic of Poland, won approval in the Bundestag. In addition, an agreement among the United States, Great Britain, France, and the USSR that reduced tensions concerning the status of West Berlin entered into force.

Apprehensions about the conceptual flaws and practical conduct of the Ostpolitik, which lingered under the chancellorship of Willy Brandt, gradually subsided after he was relieved of his office in 1974 and was replaced by his party colleague Helmut Schmidt. In the second half of the 1970s, a consensus emerged in the Federal Republic that the Ostpolitik was beneficial to West German interests and that, at any rate, there was no viable alternative to it. Changes in the international and national political climate in the early 1980s contributed to the replacement of the social-liberal coalition in October 1982 (after thirteen years in office) by a conservative-liberal combination. The new government has not renounced the Ostpolitik nor even shown an inclination to alter its substance appreciably.

My initial negative stance vis-a-vis the Ostpolitik did not prejudice me against evaluating this policy objectively as it developed. During the past half-dozen years, I have devoted a great deal of time to an exploration of the many facets of the Ostpolitik and, in the process, have come to appreciate that its introduction was inevitable and its continuation unavoidable. I am not certain if the benefits that may accrue to the Federal Republic will outweigh the liabilities it stands to incur from the Ostpolitik in the long term.

Soviet Foreign Policy in Transition
February 1971

Non-traditional Soviet-American animosity

SOVIET ATTITUDES TOWARD THE UNITED STATES

Observers as widely different as the late John Foster Dulles, secretary of state under President Eisenhower, and Michel Tatu, the eminent French journalist and editorial writer of Le Monde, have commented on an outstanding anomaly in the hostile relationship which has persisted between the Soviet Union and the United States throughout the entire postwar period. In their view, the conventional causes that have traditionally led to hostility between states--for example, territorial ambitions, ethnic grievances, and economic rivalry for markets and raw material resources--have been absent from the Soviet-American relationship. If this is so, the two countries should have been able to compose their differences, live at peace with each other, and exert their combined influences to promote peace on a global scale. Yet this has patently not been the case. The two countries have been antagonistic to each other and have exerted their efforts at cross-purposes, either to gain influence at the other's expense or to deny any advantage to the other in a given area. What is at the root of this rivalry? Tatu, writing in the Times of London early in January 1971 under the title "The U.S.: Russia's Artificial Enemy," asserts that the origin of the Soviet-American antagonism was "in a sense accidental." Two factors contributed to it: the emergence of these countries as

Tatu's theory of the accidental origin of the US-Soviet rivalry:
1.) After WW II, the only two great powers
2.) Soviet ideology made it necessary to designate the U.S. as an enemy

the only great powers in the world following the defeat
of Nazi Germany, and the militancy of the communist
ideology which made it "natural for the Soviet leaders
to designate as the supreme enemy the chief capitalist
power, whose methods and achievements were the most
evident symbol of the social regime which must be
overthrown."

Tatu's characterization of the casual origin of
the rivalry is suspect. But it is difficult to refute
the validity of his observation that the preeminence of
the two countries on the world scene has contributed
greatly to their antagonistic postures. The question
is, Would this antagonism express itself in the same
way as it has, were it not for the deep-seated ideological component underlying it? The answer is probably no.

Honest men can differ in their appraisal of the
importance that ideology plays in determining the conflict, and it is not my intent here to resolve these
differences. Suffice it to say that even the pragmatic
Tatu admits that although "Soviet diplomacy is no
longer inspired by revolutionary ideology, if it ever
was, and the repertoire of leftist slogans has lost its
persuasive force inside the country, . . . these slogans and ideology [nevertheless] continue to furnish
the Soviet leaders with their sole credentials." I
would put it somewhat differently and suggest that, at
the very minimum, the Soviet leadership has to cling to
the established Marxist-Leninist ideology to preserve
the ego-identity of the regime. Without such identification, the whole raison d'etre of the Soviet system
would vanish. In the terminology of modern political
science, we might say that the ideology is essential
for system maintenance, and that maintenance is the
most modest goal the Soviet leaders could conceivably
pursue.

The position of the United States as the foremost
adversary of Soviet Russia is thus ideologically defined, and this imparts a fixed permanence to the
adversary relationship. Within this framework, relations between the two countries can either improve or
deteriorate, but they cannot be truly friendly in our
nonideological sense of the concept of friendship.

Regardless of what their actual policies of the
moment may be, the Soviet leaders always regard the
United States as the leading imperialist power in the
world, whose very existence thwarts the ultimate fulfillment of communist goals. The United States epitomizes capitalism, just as the Soviet Union epitomizes
socialism. As a capitalist power, America is by definition imperialistic in seeking to expand its influence
primarily by economic means, in order to secure its
own economic survival. The intrinsic nature of the
capitalist system also makes it warlike. The

Soviet ideology cannot be abandoned: it is the sole raison d'etre of the leadership. even for a pragmatic reason.

Soviet-American competition reflects a permanent incompatibility between two antithetical social systems whose fundamental differences cannot be reconciled.

It is in this context that the evolution of Soviet-American relations must be examined, and it is in this sense that they must be distinguished from the Sino-Soviet conflict. This conflict now appears quite acute, and it has both ideological and conventional components (such as clashing national interests and a disputed frontier). Nevertheless, it continues to be interpreted and thus acted upon by the Soviet leaders as if it were a temporary aberration in what is otherwise, for the long historic pull, a sound, close, fraternal alliance.

To the ideological chasm that separates the United States and the Soviet Union, and the antithetical character of their respective social, economic, and political systems (which are the main determinants of their antagonistic relationship), a third basic factor of relatively recent origin must be added: their preeminence as powers in possession of an abundant arsenal of nuclear weapons. I say preeminence because they have lost the exclusiveness they once briefly shared as the only nuclear powers in the world. Their obvious superiority over all other nations--in terms of their present stock of weapons, delivery capabilities, resources, and technological know-how--still endows them with unmatched attributes.

The advent of nuclear arms technology has aggravated the Soviet-American relationship. It has for the first time raised the specter of a direct armed confrontation between them. They have become mortally vulnerable to each other's armed thrusts. By the same token, the mutuality of the threat of annihilation has forced a certain caution on them and tamed them in the practical manifestations of their conflict, lest it escalate to an irretrievable point. The impracticality of getting at each other directly has placed a greater premium on the conduct of their struggle by indirect and peaceful means.

In 1956, the Soviet leadership explicitly acknowledged that nuclear weapons sufficiency had a qualitative impact on the conduct of international relations. It was now futile to hope to win a final victory over capitalism by force of arms. It therefore became necessary to abandon this tenet of Leninism and to emphasize an equally valid doctrinal tenet, which advocates operating in the framework of peaceful coexistence between antagonistic social systems. Many observers, particularly the Chinese Communists, felt that by making such an acknowledgment the Soviet leaders were in fact writing off any notion of a final, incisive victory over capitalism. They felt the Soviets were willing to settle for something far less

satisfactory--a permanent accommodation with the dread
enemy. In the eyes of the Chinese Communists, the
Soviet leaders had lost their nerve, and that, of
course, was tantamount to forswearing their revolutionary heritage and kowtowing to the United States.

The thesis advanced by the Chinese Communists that
ultimate victory is inconceivable without an armed
clash may have some validity. But it may also be true
that a general armed clash between nuclear powers can
no longer be contemplated. It would lead to the mutual
devastation of the contestants and not to the victory
of one over the other. What this adds up to is that,
either way, the Communists might as well abandon any
realistic expectation of global hegemony. So far, we
have had no reliable indication that they have accepted
this premise and acted upon it.

The possibility of a special relationship between
the United States and Soviet Russia, leading to some
sort of nuclear condominium over the world, has been
hinted at from time to time. Although both sides
occasionally may have been tempted to enter into this
type of relationship, the fact is that they have not
done so. The chances for its consummation--if such
ever existed--are diminishing rapidly with the proliferation of nuclear weapons technology and manufacture, at least among a select number of countries,
including Communist China.

Instead of leading to a special arrangement, the
Soviet-American relationship has tended to oscillate,
sometimes quite wildly and at short intervals, between
confrontation and negotiation. It has never gone to
the limit of confrontation, that is, direct armed
clash. The Soviet leaders have been especially careful
to operate with a wide margin of safety. At worst, they
have engaged the United States military by proxy, sup-
plying arms to our foes and arming the foes of our
friends. At best, they have shunned a military showdown, even of limited scope, if it threatened to involve us or our allies. Conversely, the prospect of
negotiations has never been fully realized, and nothing
like an entente cordiale has been approached. Neither
side has yet been able to break through the barrier of
distrust which has been erected between them. This
barrier is frequently reinforced by perceptions of each
other that are filtered through their respective
prisms, tinted with a deeply ingrained ideological
bias. There is no evidence that the impetus for
breaking through this barrier has been very strong on
either side.

Contemporary Soviet-American relations conform to
the seesawing pattern of improvement/deterioration and
hope/disappointment that has been discernible since the
death of Stalin in 1953. Few will recall that in
1956 the Soviet Union, under the management of the

flamboyant Nikita S. Khrushchev, proferred a treaty
of friendship to the United States, which President
Eisenhower politely but firmly rejected as devoid of
meaningful substance.[1]

President Nixon, on taking office, proclaimed the
end of the period of confrontation and the onset of the
era of negotiations with the Soviet Union. He was
cautious in predicting rapid progress, yet optimistic
about the prospect of real achievements. In a press
conference on February 6, 1969 (shortly after his inau-
guration), the president said that he took a "dim view
of what some have called instant summitry." Nevertheless, he believed that "a well-prepared summit meeting
[with the Russians] would be in our interest and in
their interest," and it would be his intention "to see
if such a meeting could take place." He also moved to
submit the nuclear nonproliferation treaty signed in
1968 for ratification.[2] In answer to a journalist
who perceived this as a change of heart (during the
presidential campaign in fall 1968 Mr. Nixon opposed
ratification because of the Soviet invasion of Czechoslovakia), the president explained that the situation
"has changed in the sense that the number of Soviet
forces in Czechoslovakia has been substantially reduced, . . . and that the passage of time [less than
six months had elapsed] tends somewhat to reduce the
pent-up feelings that were then present with regard to
the Soviet Union's action."

The president clearly signaled to the Soviet
leadership that, despite the moral repugnance of their
violation of Czechoslovakia's integrity, the way was
open to comprehensive explorations of an improvement in
the relations between Russia and America.

A few days later, the New York Times reported that
"President Nixon and the Soviet leadership have opened
a broad dialogue on foreign policy problems that could
lead to an eventual visit to Moscow by Mr. Nixon."

The Soviet response to the president's initiative
was highly encouraging. On July 10, 1969, Andrei A.
Gromyko, the Soviet foreign minister, delivered perhaps
the most significant and wide-ranging policy review of
his long and illustrious career. He told the Supreme
Soviet of the USSR (Russia's federal parliament) that

the U.S. president's statements in favor of a
well-prepared Soviet-American summit meeting
have, of course, not gone unnoticed in the
Soviet Union. We do not cherish illusions
that the number of those against establishing
good relations between the two countries will
rapidly decline in the United States. Over
there the mechanism motivated by the forces
that do not disguise their hostility toward
our social system continues to work full

blast. But even these elements must understand that averting a clash between the
world's two largest powers and bringing about
normal or, still better, good relations between them is in the interests of both countries.

Gromyko further averred that

we are for developing good relations with the
United States and would like these relations
to be turned into friendly ones, since we are
convinced that this would be in line with the
interests of both the Soviet and American
peoples. It is clear that our two countries
are divided by deep class differences. But
the Soviet Union has always proceeded from
the premise that in questions concerning the
maintenance of peace, the USSR and the United
States can find a common language. . . . We
have noticed President Nixon's statement
that, in his opinion, the period of confrontation is followed by an era of negotiations.
The Soviet Union favors negotiations. If the
U.S. government will pursue this line in
deeds, then we on our part are ready, as
previously, to seek agreed positions on both
questions of bilateral relations . . . and
unsettled international problems.[3]

Perhaps inveterate Kremlin watchers would note the
reference to the Soviet Union's readiness "as previously" to reach accommodation, and on this basis they
would discard Gromyko's rhetoric as just that. For "as
previously" is a stock formula, connoting the immutable
correctness of the Soviet attitude and implying that
the preconditions of an agreement could be met by a
change in the attitude of Russia's negotiating partner.
Still, Gromyko's remarks sounded promising. They con-
trasted starkly with the bitter tones in which he
complained that "even our most rabid enemies have never
resorted to such unworthy methods and on such a scale
as the Chinese leaders are now doing to discredit the
activities of the Soviet Union. . . . For many years
now the Chinese leaders have been disparaging our policies." Perhaps there was a connection between the
harsh words aimed at the Chinese and the conciliatory
language directed toward the United States. To what
degree Soviet foreign policy toward America is a function of the Sino-Soviet relationship remains problematic, and there is neither the time nor the space to
explore it here in depth.
Russia's relations with Communist China have become stabilized, and the extensive armed skirmishes on

their long frontier (which were commonplace in 1969) have subsided. Yet the two countries are still at serious odds. Soviet-American relations, meanwhile, have deteriorated steadily.

A summit meeting is no longer being talked about and is not likely to take place. Instead, the president has visited Romania and Yugoslavia.[4]

Strategic arms limitation talks--begun in Helsinki in fall 1969, continued in Vienna in spring of 1970, and held again in Helsinki in fall 1970--have led to no visible result. If they are not stalemated, they are showing only glacial progress.[5]

There are, of course, good reasons why the two countries should not rush into agreements. The technical aspects of the problems involved are highly complex, and the political obstacles in the way of mutual accommodation in so sensitive an area are virtually insurmountable. As both sides probe each other more deeply, they grow frightened at the implications of a binding agreement, just as they are frightened by the possible consequences of nonagreement. The psychological hazards impeding progress are as great as are the frustrations felt at the lack of progress. No one who has not read the confidential record of the exchanges can have a clear picture of what has transpired in them, and I have not been perusing such data.

From my reading of the Soviet press, I would conclude that the Russians in principle are not averse to a reliable agreement on strategic arms. In this aim they are motivated entirely by self-interest. Since their economy is substantially smaller than ours, it would be expedient for them to reduce their military costs. It is difficult, however, to know the exact profile of their military expenditures, since their overt budget for national defense conceals more than it reveals. Less than 18 billion rubles has been allocated for the military in 1971.[6] This is a ludicrously low figure, unless a ruble buys three or four times the military power for them than a dollar does for us. On the basis of what we _do_ know about the efficiency of their economic system, it is unimaginable that this should be the case. In all likelihood, a ruble does not buy much more military power for them than a dollar does for us. (To say even this is giving them the benefit of doubt.) Thus, any reduction in military expenditures the Russians could safely project for several years would be of comparatively greater advantage to them than would be an equal reduction of costs to us. Their long-range planning would be assisted, and they could move more confidently to reallocate their relatively scarce human and material resources, in order to refurbish their economic system. Despite impressive strides, the Soviet economy lags considerably behind the American in just about every respect, particularly in the use of computer technology and modern methods of management.

While the Soviets are desirous of effecting major and rapid improvements in their economy, they are also determined not to concede any military advantage to us. What they want at the very minimum is complete parity. To achieve this, they need either to build up their forces, such as in naval armaments, or to induce us unilaterally to reduce those advantages as we may have, such as the dismantling of our foreign bases and the withdrawing of our forward, mobile, offensive air capability. They condemn our reluctance to yield to their preferences as evidence of our stubborn adherence to a discredited policy, which was developed in the 1950s by Secretary of State Dulles and was based on the notion of superior positions of strength vis-a-vis Russia.

A further indication of the present embittered state of Soviet-American relations is the extensive vilification campaign of the United States conducted by the Soviet mass media. A campaign of this sort is not without precedent, but it is unusual in its intensity and scope. One of its prongs is aimed at the alleged subversion and espionage fostered by us, which necessitates unrelenting vigilance on the part of the Soviet security organs and the whole population.

The second prong seeks to discredit our judiciary by vastly exaggerating the plight of Angela Davis. A large amount of newsprint has been lavished on her, including a plethora of pictures and illustrations, a poem dedicated to her, and letters of protest to the president of the United States signed by illustrious Soviet scientists and artists. This is out of proportion, even if due consideration is given to the fact that the Soviet press has perhaps never had as attractive and credible a victim of American "racism and lawlessness" to display before its domestic audience. In fact, Miss Davis is the first flesh-and-blood black American Communist whose cause the Soviet press could champion. Other Communists have not been nearly as attractive, and although blacks have been affiliated with the Communist party, their number has been insignificant.

The third prong consists of accusations against the U.S. government of aiding and abetting not only Israeli aggression in the Middle East but Zionist excesses against Soviet installations and representatives on American territory. Soviet media claim that these excesses could not take place without collusion and encouragement on the part of the government. By way of retaliation, the Soviet government not only castigates us but mobilizes popular protest meetings with conspicuous participation by loyal Soviet Jews. It also organizes a selective, little-publicized terror campaign against U.S. diplomatic personnel and press correspondents.

Minimum Soviet bid: virtual parity achieved either by arms build up or by unilateral U.S. army reduction

Soviet needling & anti-U.S. bias:
1.) U.S. subversion & underdevelopment in USSR

2.) U.S. domestic attacks on leftists and minorities (ie. Angela Davis)

3.) Accuses U.S. of abetting Israeli aggression and Zionist excesses in USSR

Some aspects of this vilification campaign clearly cater to domestic needs. Warnings against the pervasiveness of American subversion and espionage are part of a broader effort, designed to legitimize the need for ubiquitous vigilance and to refurbish the tarnished image of the security organs of the country. Beyond that, the unmistakable message of the vilification campaign is cautionary, lest the citizenry (and possibly even segments of Soviet officialdom) get carried away with undue hopes of a meaningful relaxation of tensions with the United States. It may well be that the whole Soviet political leadership, or perhaps a significant portion of it (consisting of party hardliners, the military, and the secret police--a counterpart of our so-called military-industrial complex), harbors genuine concerns over a potential weakening of resolve in the ongoing struggle with the United States.

The truculence that is manifest toward us may be in large part, if not wholly, self-generated and self-serving. It may be related, among other things, to behind-the-scenes skirmishing in advance of the Twenty-fourth Congress of the Communist party of the Soviet Union (CPSU), which is scheduled to open on March 30, 1971. This would not be the first instance in which domestic considerations were paramount in determining foreign policy. The Soviet leaders are free from the political constraints which are imposed on policy makers in a democratic system by a need to gain and retain the favor of the electorate. They do not have to devise their foreign policy with a view toward maximizing their chances of being returned to office, as does, say, the president of the United States. Nevertheless, they cannot be oblivious to the disposition of certain constituencies, especially within the ruling hierarchy of the party and in the military, nor can they be unmindful of the economic and social necessities of the population.

In any event, whether it is by choice or necessity, the large amount of hostility shown the United States by the Soviet mass media does not augur favorably for an early and significant improvement in the relations between the two countries. A survey of both American and Soviet policy initiatives throughout the world also confirms this conclusion. There is no area, whether it be Europe or the Middle East, Southeast Asia or Latin America, in which the Soviet Union and the United States are proceeding in concert.

SOVIET POLICIES IN EUROPE

Europe has been the traditional area in which Soviet policy has asserted itself. Although the Soviet Union has global ambitions and operates on a global scale, it is in Europe that Soviet policy has been most dynamic. For Russia, despite the vastness of its

Siberian expanse and the importance of its Central
Asian republics, is to all intents and purposes a
European power. It knows Europe best, and its destiny
is inextricably linked with that of Europe. Gromyko,
in the policy speech from which I have already quoted,
said: "More often than not the fate of our country has
been dependent on the development of events in Europe.
In other words, the security of the Soviet Union is in-
separable from all-European security."

The year 1970 will be remembered as a year in
which the Soviet Union once again turned to Europe as
the central arena of its foreign policy initiatives.
The major thrust of its efforts was directed at the
Federal Republic of Germany, with which it concluded a
treaty on August 12, 1970. Other significant developments included a visit to Moscow by French President
Georges Pompidou, which served to reaffirm the close
working relationship established under the late President Charles de Gaulle; a visit to Italy by Soviet
Foreign Minister Gromyko, which set the stage for a
further expansion of economic contacts; and an unrelenting championing of a European security conference
to be held at the earliest possible opportunity.

Two questions need to be answered. Why the turn
to Europe in 1970 and what has been accomplished?

Some analysts have suggested that the stabilization of conditions in Europe, which appears to be a
Soviet goal, is essential for Russia to be able to deal
incisively with the acute crisis it faces in the Far
East. Others have maintained that, on the contrary,
the Soviet Union's success in stabilizing the Far Eastern situation has permitted it to become more dynamic
and aggressive in Europe.

There can be no doubt of the interrelatedness
between conditions on Russia's Eastern and Western
borders. What some analysts have thought to be a
geopolitical advantage is in fact a serious disadvantage for the Soviet Union under present circumstances. The USSR straddles two continents and domi-
nates the heartland of the world. But does it have
adequate internal lines of communications, and can it
bring superior power to bear against two distinct opponents, one situated to the West and one to the East?
And what about the demographic balance in Asia, if not
in Europe? Thus, the Soviet Union must view with
apprehension the prospect of simultaneous embroilment
on two fronts, and it must seek to stabilize one in
order to be free to act on the other. Stalin acted on
this premise in April 1941 when he concluded a neutrality treaty with hostile Japan. There is no reason
for the present leaders in the Kremlin to act differently.

Quite apart from these concerns and the diagnosis
that may be based on them, the long-range interests of

1969 FRG elections. SDs with the Ostpolitik
win and Brandts at the helm. An opportunity
for the Soviets to penetrate into Western Europe
has arisen.

13

the Soviet Union need be taken into account in ana-
lyzing its latest policy gambits. A stable, protected
border in the West has been an immutable Soviet objective. Beyond that the Russians have never really
stopped looking for an opportunity to penetrate the
West peacefully and gradually. At least for the time
being, anything more ambitious would be out of the
question. Thus, even if the inflamed conditions in the
Far East imparted a sense of urgency to the search for
an opening in Europe, this search did not necessitate
an adaptation in the framework of Soviet policies on
the European continent. The real opportunity to make
any headway was provided by the German federal elections in September 1969, which brought to power a
coalition government headed by the Social Democratic
party and committed to a new Ostpolitik.

The Soviet Union may have anticipated this turn of
events, for Gromyko, in his speech to which I again
make reference, told the West Germans that

> there may be a change in our relations. . . .
> For this, the plans of revenge for the last
> war must give way to the realization that the
> future of the Federal Republic of Germany,
> with its considerable technical and economic
> capabilities, lies in peaceful cooperation
> with all states, including the Soviet Union.
> Proceeding from these premises, the
> Soviet government is prepared to continue an
> exchange of views with the Federal Republic
> of Germany on the renunciation of the use of
> force, including the conclusion of an appro-
> priate agreement.

The Soviet-German treaty itself is unspectacular.
In essence, it commits both parties to the renunciation
of force in dealing with each other. It also confirms
their acceptance of the inviolability, now and in the
future, of the frontiers of "all states in Europe, as
they are on the day of signing of this treaty, including the Oder-Neisse line, which forms the western frontier of the Polish People's Republic, and the frontier
between the Federal Republic of Germany and the German
Democratic Republic."

The innocent language of the treaty has many
troubling connotations. Basically, it sanctifies the
Potsdam Agreements of 1945—and thus the division of
Europe—which the Russians have steadfastly upheld as
the cornerstone of the postwar international order on
the continent. It lays to rest any lingering hope of
the unification of Germany into a single state, and
puts all of Eastern Europe out of the reach of would-be
German meddling. Furthermore, the political under-
standings attendant upon the treaty give encouragement

Soviet-FRG Treaty permanizes the
temporary Potsdam arrangements

to a dialogue between East and West Germans on the
basis of formal equality, and they jeopardize the delicate status of West Berlin.

By no stretch of the imagination have the Russians
indicated willingness to modify their position on Berlin. This position was spelled out by Leonid I.
Brezhnev, secretary general of the CPSU, in Yerevan,
the capital of Soviet Armenia, on November 29, 1970.
On numerous occasions since, Soviet spokesmen have
referred to his speech as a faithful reflection of all
that could be expected from the Soviet Union. In
Mr. Brezhnev's words:

> We hold that normalization of the situation
> in relation to West Berlin is quite achiev-
> able. All that is required is that all par-
> ties concerned should show good will and work
> out decisions which would meet the wishes of
> the West Berlin population and take account
> of the legitimate interests and sovereign
> rights of the German Democratic Republic.[7]

What does this imply? For example, are the legitimate interests and sovereign rights of the German
Democratic Republic, as seen by the Russians, compatible with the continued Federal German political presence in West Berlin? And if not, can the West Germans, for psychological and morale reasons, abandon
their claim to this presence? How can this issue be
resolved? And what pressures on the West Germans will
be generated by the conditions they themselves set for
an agreement on West Berlin, prior to the ratification
of the Soviet-German treaty?[8]

Not all the ramifications of the treaty can be
enumerated here, let alone analyzed in detail. It is
obvious, however, that the Soviet Union scored a signal
success. It has gained leverage within West Germany.
This is evident from the mounting turmoil occasioned by
the dissatisfaction of the internal opposition with
Chancellor Willy Brandt's Eastern policy, and by the
uncertainties engendered by the lack of minute specifications of the obligations and intentions of the signatories, in regard to a host of pertinent domestic and
international issues. German-American relations have
been somewhat shaken. At least a segment of American
opinion has lost confidence in the reliability of our
West German allies. The Federal German government has
been put on the defensive. It has found it necessary
to explain itself both to its domestic and foreign
critics, to reassure its constituents that in signing
the treaty it was not following a will-of-the-wisp, and
to counter rumors that the Soviet Union has already
lost interest in the treaty. That a rumor of this sort
can even gain currency is indicative of the nervousness
prevailing in West Germany. It should be clear to all

that in the Soviet scheme of things the German treaty occupies an important position, and this scheme is both stable and well thought-out.

Soviet interests in Europe are many and varied. Some may be out-of-reach for the Russians, and others may take many years to achieve; but the Russians are in no hurry. They are moving deliberately under the guise of a peaceful penetration of the West, in concert with many groups of good will, fostering what in the 1930s were called "popular front" tactics. These called for cooperation among communists, socialists, liberals, and just about anyone who then opposed fascism. The purpose of the current variant of popular fronts would be to expel from the continent the common enemy of all Europeans--America.

The initial vehicle by which Europeans are to assert their solidarity, their common aims, and their reliance on one another is a security conference. The idea is not novel. The conclusion of a European security treaty was first broached by Vyacheslav M. Molotov, then minister of foreign affairs of the Soviet Union, at a Foreign Ministers Conference held in Berlin in January and February 1954. Molotov's plan relegated the United States to observer status in a European security system, along with the People's Republic of China. In his report on this conference, Mr. Dulles, the American secretary of state, characterized the Soviet position as preposterous and said "laughter rippled" among Western delegates on hearing Mr. Molotov's proposal.[9] In the face of such a cool reception the plan was shelved. It was resuscitated without substantive changes in 1966 at a meeting of the Warsaw Pact countries in Bucharest and has been assiduously promoted since then. In 1969, the Russians succeeded in persuading the Finnish government to assume responsibility for sponsoring this project.

A conference on European security attended by European states only would not necessarily represent a major threat to existing treaty arrangements, which hold Russia at bay and promote West European cooperation. But it might represent a small chink in the West's psychological, if not military, defenses, and this alone appears to make its convocation worthwhile from the Soviet point of view. Lest one grow disdainful of such modest expectations, it is well to remind oneself that the echoes of the laughter which rippled through the ranks of Western delegates in 1954 upon learning Russia's plans for a European security conference have long since subsided. Instead, one hears the president of France paying at least lip service if not more to the idea. It is an almost imperceptible change. Can one safely ignore it?[10]

In 1970, the Russians made an auspicious start in their new phase of peaceful penetration of Western Europe. The same cannot be said about our attempts at

peaceful engagement in Eastern Europe. Although the
Soviet Union has experienced enormous difficulties in
subordinating to its will the small, hapless countries
of Eastern Europe (and on several occasions has even
been humiliated by them), it has managed to uphold the
validity of its supremacy in this area. There have
been no incursions into Eastern Europe by the West.
Thrice the Soviet Union has had to resort to the use of
massive military power to keep its unruly vassals in
line: in 1953 in East Germany, in 1956 in Hungary, and
in 1968 in Czechoslovakia. Thrice the West stood idle,
thereby confirming the legitimacy of Russia's claim to
the fealty of these regimes.

The intervention of the Warsaw Pact powers in
Czechoslovakia in August 1968 continues to be labeled
as a political defeat for the Soviet Union. True, it
was a move dictated by necessity rather than choice.
But its consequences have been so felicitous for the
Russians that it can be called a defeat only at the
risk of deceiving oneself. The military occupation of
Czechoslovakia was an essential prerequisite of the
successful launching of the present campaign of peaceful penetration of Western Europe. It effectively
plugged a hole in the Warsaw Pact's defenses and
thereby contributed to a sense of security in the East,
as had the erection of the Berlin Wall in 1961.

With Soviet troops deployed in strength in forward
positions all along the crucial demarcation line in
Europe, a glacis was consolidated. Soviet troops now
patrolled a frontier on which they had not before
stood. This was bound to have an effect on West Germany, causing it to rethink the premises of its Eastern
policy, which were predicated on the isolation of East
Germany from the rest of the Warsaw Pact countries.
The West Germans instead had to abide by Russia's
priorities, sign a treaty with the Soviet Union before
coming to an agreement with any other East European
state, and abandon any plans for isolating East Germany. Mr. Brezhnev had good reason to crow, as he did
on November 24, 1970, at the Tenth Congress of the Hungarian Socialist Workers party in Budapest, that "the
conclusion of the treaty [with West Germany] was . . .
the outcome of the many-year-long coordinated, prin-
cipled policy of our community."

SOVIET POLICIES IN THE MIDDLE EAST

In the Middle East, the Soviet Union has skillfully exploited the conflict between the Arab states
and Israel to its advantage. By supporting the Arab
states, the Russians have maximized their opportunities
of penetrating the area geographically and gaining some
influence over the vital resource of the region--oil.
There can be no doubt that the interests of the Soviet

leaders are not limited to the Middle Eastern region proper nor to the achievement of preponderant influence over the Arab states. Rather, the Middle East is a staging area from which it is possible to threaten the fuel supply of Western Europe; interfere with navigation on one of the world's most important commercial waterways, the Suez Canal; transform the eastern Mediterranean into something close to a Soviet mare nostrum; and, if necessary, envelop the Southern flank of NATO.

Less than twenty years ago the Soviet presence in the Middle East was hardly felt. Today it is the dominant feature in the international relations and even the domestic politics of many of the states in this area.

The expansion of Soviet influence in the area proper was aided by some grievous miscalculations on the part of Western statesmen. Yet the Soviet Union also made mistakes, and the growth of its influence has not been sustained. It suffered serious setbacks as a consequence of Israel's resounding military successes in 1956 and 1967. Apart from the loss of military equipment estimated at several billion dollars, Soviet prestige was also lowered. The only redeeming element of these defeats was an increased dependence of the Arab states on Soviet assistance. Another source of difficulty for Russia has been the internal instability of several Arab regimes. This has impeded attempts to transform them into dependable client states and has necessitated the exertion of repeated efforts to establish close working relations with their new leaders. Finally, the Russians have had to contend with the competing appeal of Maoist revolutionary ideology and such assistance as Communist China has given to radical elements among dispossessed Palestinian Arabs.

Two significant developments helped the Soviet Union in 1970. The first event was the deep penetration bombing of Egypt carried out by Israel in the early part of the year. It gave rise to a frenzied plea by President Gamal Abdel Nasser for increased Soviet military aid, which brought to Egypt not only sophisticated weaponry but Soviet personnel in significant numbers to man it. It is not likely that the intent of the Soviet Union was to escalate the danger of war. Russia has little to gain from a third military go-around, and another defeat may have devastating direct consequences for the Soviet military establishment. On the other hand, the threat of a victory over Israel would probably trigger U.S. participation in the fray, and the Russians have shown no willingness to enter into a direct test of arms with us. Thus, the purposes of shoring up Egypt's defenses were to overcome that country's chronic military inferiority vis-a-vis Israel; to restore its self-confidence, which

is indispensable for the conduct of negotiations over a
political settlement; and, most importantly, to tighten
Russia's grip on the United Arab Republic. It would
appear that these objectives have been substantially
achieved.

Another event the Soviet Union has sought to turn
to its advantage was President Nasser's sudden death in
September 1970. At first this seemed like a blow to
Soviet interests, for Nasser was the best and most
reliable friend Russia had in the Middle East and his
preeminence among Arab leaders was an asset. But by
virtue of being a truly charismatic leader he hindered
a deeper penetration of Egypt's political infrastructure. Following his death, therefore, the opportunity
for further penetration presented itself. His successor Anwar Sadat does not now have Nasser's charisma and
could not, in the context of the domestic political and
psychological climate, immediately aspire to it. The
Russians wasted no time in initiating closer contacts
between the CPSU and the Arab Socialist Union of Egypt,
in the expectation that it would become an increasingly
important political vehicle.

In December 1970, a large Soviet delegation headed
by Boris N. Ponomarev, a secretary of the Central
Committee of the CPSU, was dispatched to Egypt. The
length of its stay there, the scope of its activities,
and not least the composition of its personnel attested
to the importance attached by the Soviet leadership to
this mission. For Ponomarev is not only a very high-
ranking party official, he is also one of the oldest
and shrewdest operatives, whose service began in the
Communist International under Stalin. A similar effort
to expand and improve relations with the new leadership
of the Syrian Arab Republic is now also underway.

The American peace initiative in the summer of
1970 could not be ignored nor an answer to it long
delayed by the Russians and their allies. The timing
of the initiative, however, was not felicitous for them
since they had not yet fully deployed their missiles on
the West bank of the Suez Canal. Hence, they encour-
aged their friends to accept, and they proceeded to
install their missiles at the risk of provoking an
outraged reaction by Israel.

The American peace initiative irritated the Russians for other reasons as well. High-ranking administration spokesmen made it clear that the real thrust of
our peace effort was to expel the Soviet Union from its
forward positions in the Middle East. This, of course,
is unacceptable to the Soviet Union. It will simply
not enter into any kind of agreement that would diminish the influence it has laboriously developed. For
the time being, the Russians seem to have the upper
hand. They are in process of entrenching themselves
in Arab states and are using the leverage provided by

Israel's intractable position to make headway in this endeavor. We, by contrast, are increasingly forced to identify ourselves with Israel's basic concern over sheer survival, and in the process we are losing our remaining leverage on the Arab states, in which we have more than a perfunctory economic interest.[11]

SOVIET-AMERICAN INTEREST IN SOUTHEAST ASIA AND LATIN AMERICA

A survey of American and Soviet interests and policies in Europe and in the Middle East shows the two powers at loggerheads with each other. A brief look at Southeast Asia and Latin America reveals a similar picture, although the terms on which they are involved in these areas are very different. In Southeast Asia, the Soviet Union has for long kept a relatively low profile. In effect, it has allowed us to do the dirty work by keeping at bay virulent insurrectionary communist movements which have a close affinity for Mao's China. An international settlement in which preferably the Soviet Union would participate, but which would at least safeguard Soviet interests by denying preponderant influence to another power in the area, would probably be entirely acceptable to the Kremlin leaders. The more consistent our policies are with achieving this goal, the less vocal is the Soviet Union in denouncing our purposes in Southeast Asia. Conversely, the more we depart from a path that in the view of the Soviet leaders would enhance the chances of such an international settlement, the more irritated they are with us.

In Latin America, the Soviet Union has not established a conspicuous presence, despite the fact that it has for better than a decade supported Fidel Castro's self-styled Cuban socialism in the hope of eventually transforming it into a disciplined Soviet-style system. Soviet-Cuban relations have had their ups and downs. Cuba, of course, is potentially (if not at present actually) an important forward base for political and military activity in the Western Hemisphere. But the appeal of the Cuban revolution has been limited. On the continent itself, the Soviet Union has been operating against great odds and has just begun to develop closer relations with a few countries. The most important of these is Chile, which has recently elected a Marxist president. The Soviet press termed Salvador Allende's election as a watershed in Latin American politics, and it may be that this assessment deserves better than to be dismissed as mere propaganda. The high degree of Soviet interest in Chilean developments, which bear the mark of popular front politics, is perhaps evident in the dispatch of Sharaf R. Rashidov to attend the congress of President Allende's Socialist

party. Rashidov is first secretary of the Communist
party in Uzbekistan and an alternate member of the
Politburo. High-ranking Communist officials as a rule
do not attend congresses of noncommunist parties.

CONCLUSIONS

It is difficult and perhaps futile to attempt a
balance sheet of Soviet-American relations. Many more
factors would have to be considered than have been
explored here. However, the conclusion is inescapable
that for the moment the Soviet Union has the initiative
in Europe and is in ascendancy in the Middle East.
Particularly in Europe, the positional advantage which
the Soviet Union now seeks to improve need not be
alarming. There is no imminent threat to our security
interests nor even to that of our allies. NATO's
defenses are not in danger of being breached, and the
European Economic Community has, perhaps, gathered
enough momentum to lead to the creation of an integrated regional economic and political unit that could
interdict Soviet encroachment on it. Nor is there any
evidence that the Soviet Union is laboring under the
illusion of an easy conquest of Western Europe. The
economic contacts it seeks are dictated to a large
measure by a domestic necessity for improved technology
and credits. These contacts are predicated on an old
Leninist formula: Seek the help of Western capitalists
whenever it is to the benefit of the Soviet system. In
a political sense, it is unlikely that the ambitions of
the Soviet leadership for the foreseeable future--ten
to twenty years hence--envisage anything more radical
than the emergence in Western Europe of "a series of
larger Finlands." That in itself would be a development we could not contemplate equanimously.
In the pursuit of their objectives, the Soviet
leaders have shown remarkable persistence and very
little propensity for departing from what they call
Leninist norms. These, of course, permit a considerable range of policy analyses and provide for a broad
spectrum of strategic and tactical options. An almost
infinite flexibility of strategy and tactics is the
hallmark of Leninism. It is well to keep this in mind.
From the perusal of public sources (and that is all
that an academician has at his disposal), the evidence
is overwhelming that basic foreign policy analysis in
the Soviet Union continues to recognize the Leninist
categories of conflict: class contradictions; inter-
capitalist rivalry; conflict between metropolitan countries and their colonies; and, finally, the socialist-
capitalist antagonism. (Provisions are lacking for a
fifth category of conflict between socialist systems,
for the underlying causes of contradictions are by
definition eliminated when the transition is made from

capitalism to socialism, that is, from an exploitative type of economy with private ownership to a non-exploitative economy with social ownership.)

There is also strong evidence that the Soviet leaders think in dialectical terms, by force of habit if for no other reason. They tend to see a definite, objectively determined causality between events, and they have a dynamic rather than static view of international relations. They do not shun conflict, for it is an essential element in the dialectical process. They project international relations on a scale of continuous conflict, which can range from relatively harmless clashes in the realm of peace to very dangerous confrontations in the realm of war. War and peace are but different modes of conflict.

Contrary to the claims they advance, their "scientific" analysis of the moving forces of world history does not provide them with infallible insights. Often they err in not making the proper analysis and not grasping, for purposes of policy implementation, what they call the "next link" in the chain of events. International relations are not quite as susceptible to an orderly analysis, cast in rigid categories, as the Communists would like them to be. But if the quality of Soviet foreign policy is not superior to that of any other state, it has certain permanent characteristics. Knowledge of these may be helpful in avoiding a sense of bewilderment at seemingly incomprehensible turns in Soviet policy (they are probably understandable in dialectical terms) and in anticipating the unfolding of Soviet strategic designs. For example, many people tend to be misled by the Soviet's avowal to be following a policy of detente. To most of us, detente implies a static condition in which international tensions are relaxed, if not wholly eliminated. To the Russians, detente is not necessarily an end in itself but a means by which they can either better prepare for or actually pursue an expansionist strategy.

The alleged mediocrity of the present Soviet leadership should be carefully scrutinized. With the exception of Lenin, the top Soviet leaders--Stalin, Khrushchev, and the current troika of Brezhnev, Kosygin and Podgorny--have all been described as mediocre. Yet their achievements have not been negligible. Khrushchev tended to be the most innovative, and it is interesting to note that, after a relatively short period, virtually the whole Soviet hierarchy closed ranks against him. In ousting him from office they accused him of having hatched hare-brained schemes. This says something about the cast of mind of the present leaders. Their horizons are limited, their outlook parochial. Brezhnev's is perhaps more so than Kosygin's, but the difference is one of degree, not kind. It is foolish to attribute to Kosygin a sort of

familiar cosmopolitan pragmatism. He probably does not
have it; if he does, he would have to conceal it
carefully in the policy deliberations of the Politburo.
    Why should the Soviet leaders not be doctrinaire?
What in their long experiences would make them otherwise? Do men transcend their limitations at an advanced age? Do they throw off the habits of thought
and action ingrained in them throughout a lifetime? In
dealing with the Soviet leaders, it is advisable to
keep certain caveats in mind and not to exaggerate the
likelihood--as some of our representatives in the recent past have--of their tractability.
    Younger men, among whom Kirill T. Mazurov,
Dmitriy S. Polyanskiy, and Alexander N. Shelepin stand
out, may be bidding for power. (Some of them may have
replaced one or another of their elders in the leadership by the time this presentation is printed.) In
what way do they differ from the present troika? Not
in any essentials. If anything, they are tougher
still. Their rise to preeminence now or later would
give scant hope for a better understanding. Mazurov,
born in 1914, joined the party in 1940, the same year
as Shelepin who is four years his junior; while
Polyanskiy, who was born in 1917, became a member of
the party in 1939.[12]
    They are not exactly babes in the woods. The
youngest is fifty-three years of age, and all have
thirty years of political experience or more. Critical
of a certain indecisiveness in current policies, they
may be attracted to the Stalinist model. Adapting it
to eliminate some of its most objectionable aspects,
they may nevertheless revive its fundamental mobiliza-
tional and coercive features, relying heavily on tight
central controls and strong discipline to infuse a
greater dynamism and purposiveness into the Soviet
system.
    Along with a strong element of continuity in the
character of the Soviet leadership, there is also a
continuity in the relative world position of the Soviet
Union. That position has consistently been one of
inferiority vis-a-vis its opponents. The Soviet Union
has been a traditional underdog (or runner-up, as the
case may be) and has been strongly motivated to catch
up with and surpass its adversaries. The doggedness
that characterized Soviet policies in the early 1920s,
when on a world scale Soviet power was considered
infinitesimal indeed, continues to assert itself,
although Soviet power in absolute terms has grown im-
measurably. There is no evidence to support the belief
held by some that the Soviet Union has as yet tired of
its Sisyphean labor.
    Despite its accomplishments and the favorable
field position it has in Europe and the Middle East,
the Soviet Union faces further uphill struggles. In
the three-cornered competition among giants on the

world scene (which has from an Orwellian fantasy become a palpable reality), the Soviet Union is the least favored. It must compete in two very different spheres of action: that of the elemental revolution of under-developed peoples carried on by primitive means of combat, and that of the scientific-technological revolution carried on by the most sophisticated methods of research and development. Neither the United States nor China have equal obligations. China is the champion of the elemental revolution of backward peoples, and the United States is the champion and foremost exponent of the scientific-technological revolution.

To carry on in both spheres of action with equal vigor is beyond the ken of the Soviet Union. Thus, without abandoning its claims to leadership in the "anti-imperialist struggle of peoples," it has chosen to concentrate its efforts on scientific and techno-logical achievements, which it considers decisive in determining the global competition for power and in-fluence.

In the military application of the scientific-technological revolution, the Soviet Union started at a disadvantage and set its sights on pulling even with the United States. At the same time, it has not aban-doned all aspirations of gaining a superiority of arms, if not in absolute terms and on a world scale, then in terms of a partial, differential advantage in specific geographic areas. This could conceivably be exploited, not to force war on us but precisely the opposite, to induce us to capitulate because of the threat of war-- in other words, by political blackmail. The chances of succeeding in this sort of effort now seem remote. The threat of Armageddon is not imminent. But mili-tary power and power of the military play an increas-ingly important part in shaping the destinies of na-tions.

NOTES

1. Paul E. Zinner, ed., <u>Documents on American For-eign Relations, 1956</u> (New York: Harper and Bros. for the Council on Foreign Relations, 1957), 221-24.

2. The United States Senate approved the nuclear nonproliferation treaty on March 13, 1969, by a vote of 83 to 15.

3. <u>Pravda</u>, July 11, 1969. An authentic Soviet English language text appeared in <u>Moscow News</u>, Supple-ment to issue no. 29 (1969).

4. Despite the escalation of the Vietnam War, ordered by President Nixon shortly before his scheduled trip to the Soviet Union, a summit meeting between him and Secretary Brezhnev (who then did not yet have the title of chairman of the Presidium of the Supreme Soviet) took place in Moscow in May 1972.

5. An interim agreement between the United States
of America and the Union of Soviet Socialist Republics
on certain measures with respect to the limitation of
strategic offensive arms (SALT I) was concluded on the
occasion of President Nixon's visit in Moscow on
May 26, 1972.

6. Soviet military expenditures were estimated to
have grown at an annual rate of 4-5 percent throughout
the 1970s and to have constituted between 12-15 percent
of the gross national product (GNP), as calculated in
the Soviet Union. In off-the-record discussions, Soviet spokesmen have on occasion not disputed the accuracy of these estimates. During this entire period,
the published figures for national defense costs
hovered around the 17 billion ruble mark. They thus
represented not only a much smaller fraction of the
GNP, but a diminishing proportion of the yearly budget.

7. Pravda, November 30, 1970.

8. Actually, the Four Power Agreement on Berlin is
not a bad bargain for the Federal Republic of Germany.
But it tends to induce a certain pliancy in the policy
of the Federal Republic toward the East (particularly
toward the German Democratic Republic) in order not to
jeopardize the relief from constant harassment that has
been obtained for West Berlin. Although the terms of
the Berlin agreement harbor many tacit agreements and
disagreements, as the case may be, and include many
anomalies, they have transformed the city from a
perennial flash point in East-West relations into an
oasis of calm. By the same token, West Berlin has been
stripped of the attributes it had as a symbol of
freedom that militantly defied Soviet-Communist
tyranny. Thus, West Berlin has been deprived of its
raison d'etre and has not been able to find a new
identity. From being a political asset.to the Federal
Republic it has become an economic liability, which
drains the resources of the Federal treasury of more
than DM 10 billion a year. It has entered a period of
decline, the outcome of which is not in sight.

9. Peter V. Curl, ed., Documents on American
Foreign Relations, 1954 (New York: Harper and Bros.
for the Council on Foreign Relations, 1955), 222.

10. The Conference on Security and Cooperation in
Europe (CSCE) was one of the major vehicles which the
Soviet Union promoted for establishing standards of
international conduct among thirty-five participating
countries, including thirty-three European and two
North American powers. The scheme that Molotov had
originally proposed was not realized. The United
States, far from being relegated to observer status,
played a prominent part in the preparatory talks and
was drawn still more deeply into European affairs.

11. The Soviet Union's loss of influence in Egypt
(the most important Arab state in the area by far) was

climaxed by the expulsion from that country of Soviet
military advisors in 1972. The Kremlin had made the
mistake of championing Ali Sabry as Nasser's successor.
Sabry was Sadat's rival for this position. The Soviet
Union did not ingratiate itself to Sadat and had to pay
dearly for its miscalculation. With the aid of this
sort of development, the United States did succeed, if
not in expelling the Soviet Union from its forward
positions in the Middle East, then at least in helping
to bring about a reduction in Soviet influence in
certain crucial areas in the Middle East. The reces-
sion of Soviet power in this area from the high point
it had reached in the late 1960s and early 1970s is one
of the more blatant failures which Soviet foreign
policy sustained in the period of detente. The situation in the Middle East, however, remains in flux. The
United States appears to have made good headway in
extricating itself from an isolated position of identification with Israeli concerns for survival, but the
support it has among Arab states to secure peace in
this volatile area is not necessarily either stable or
lasting. The Soviet Union, meanwhile, has labored assiduously to reestablish a foothold in the area.

    12. Shelepin, who appeared to be the brashest of
the young Politburo members, was first to fall into
disfavor. He lost his position in the Politburo in
April 1975 and "resigned" a month later from the chairmanship of the trade unions. He was also dropped from
the Central Committee of the CPSU and disappeared from
sight. Polyanskiy fared a bit better. He lost his
Politburo seat at the Twenty-fifth Congress of the CPSU
in February 1976, but he was appointed ambassador to
Japan and retained his seat in the Central Committee
for five years. Although no longer a member of the
Central Committee, he is at this writing the Soviet
ambassador to Norway.

    Mazurov held on to his Politburo seat until Novem-
ber 1978 and was also first deputy chairman of the
Council of Ministers, next in line for the chairmanship
of the Soviet government in the event that Alexei
Kosygin relinquished that position. He was relieved of
his offices before he had a chance to succeed Kosygin.
His place in the Soviet hierarchy was taken by Nikolai
Tikhonov, a man nine years his senior. It might be
said that Tikhonov, who was born in 1905, was a "late
bloomer." He joined Mazurov as first deputy chairman
of the Council of Ministers only in 1976 and became an
alternate member of the Politburo in November 1978, at
the venerable age of seventy-three. He has since become chairman of the Council of Ministers and, of
course, has risen to full membership in the Politburo.

2
Problems and Prospects of Troop Reductions in Central Europe

The impetus to investigate the Mutual and Balanced Force Reduction (MBFR) talks in Vienna grew from an acute sense of frustration I felt at the abysmal lack of information about the negotiations in American mass media and also in the specialized literature. My intent was to learn at the negotiating site from those intimately involved in the proceedings how they viewed the underlying motivations and objectives of the participating countries, what the major issues were, and how much progress they had registered to date.

It was not my purpose to trace the convoluted history of the negotiations since their gestation stage, long before the beginning of preparatory talks in Vienna in 1973. My observations and conclusions are based principally on information obtained in discussions with either the chief delegates or their deputies (and in some instances both) representing the eleven directly participating countries (the United States, the United Kingdom, Canada, the Federal Republic of Germany, Belgium, Luxembourg, the Netherlands, the Soviet Union, Poland, Czechoslovakia, and the German Democratic Republic), and with the chief delegates of three of the eight special participants (Romania, Italy, and Turkey). (Special participants are countries which are outside the designated area of reduction in Central Europe and which have no military forces in the reduction area. The other five special participants are Norway, Denmark, Greece, Hungary, and Bulgaria.) To buttress the information thus obtained, I conferred with officials in the Ministry of Foreign Affairs in Bonn and in the Department of State in Washington. For background, I perused voluminous files of unclassified documents, newspaper accounts, and other European secondary sources.

As things have turned out, the comments I made in 1977 shed light on the MBFR talks in mid-passage. While some issues to which I made reference have been resolved in the intervening years, other problems have so far proved intractable. For a time the talks were at a virtual standstill, but since early 1982 they have registered a certain degree of movement. The two sides have exchanged new proposals. The latest of these was introduced by the Warsaw Pact in the summer of 1983 and represents a significant advance over past Eastern proposals, which in the main were artful restatements of positions which the West had steadfastly rejected. With an appropriate response from NATO and additional concessions by the Warsaw Pact, the obstacles that bar the conclusion of a first agreement could be eliminated.

An early breakthrough in Vienna, however, remains as problematic as ever. Interest in troop withdrawal in Central Europe has long been overshadowed by concern over the proliferation of "grey area" nuclear weapons. Unless the United States and the Soviet Union manage to resolve their differences about intermediate-range nuclear forces (INF), the prospects for MBFR will be dim. In my opinion, it is as regrettable now as it was in 1977 that other arms control negotiations take precedence over the MBFR talks. Then it was SALT II; now it is INF. The urgency of reaching an MBFR agreement has not diminished. Awesome as nuclear weapons are, their use for military purposes, especially in a heavily populated industrial area like Central Europe, is improbable. Should there be war, it is likely to be fought by conventional forces, massed in unprecedented numbers in and around this area. An agreement stabilizing conventional Warsaw Pact and NATO military force relations in the center of Europe would contribute to a reduction of tensions on the entire continent. To attain this objective would seem to be worthy of the highest priority.

Observations about the Vienna Negotiations on Mutual and Balanced Force Reductions
December 1977

GENERAL OBSERVATIONS

The negotiations, variously referred to as MBFR or MFR,[1] are now entering their fifth year. Their subject matter is properly reflected in their official title and corresponding acronym--Mutual Reduction of Forces and Armaments and Associated Measures in Central Europe (MUREFAAMCE).

The complexity of these negotiations exceeds that of the strategic arms limitation talks. Whereas in SALT II two participants are involved face-to-face, in

Structure of MBFR talks: 19 participants can be divided into two blocs. While the WTO has no problem reaching a consensus, it is very difficult for the NATO bloc.

29

MBFR nineteen participants are engaged in unprecedented alliance or bloc-to-bloc negotiations, which require the elaboration of multilaterally agreed-on, unified positions before they can be presented to the other side for consideration. While this may not impose particular hardships on the Warsaw Pact, it is at the very least cumbersome and time-consuming for NATO. The subject matter of MBFR, though often regarded as less important than SALT, is of unsurpassed significance. It deals with the greatest peacetime concentration of military forces known to history, numbering approximately one million heavily armed troops on each side, deployed in an area of traditional power rivalry where two world wars were spawned and fought. Despite a protracted period of peace since 1945, the legacy of mutual suspicions and threat perceptions persists. Moreover, the reduction of essentially conventional military forces is more complicated than the resolution of problems attendant upon strategic arms. The latter can be discussed in a highly structured abstract framework, since there have been no nuclear wars. The former does not command an informing doctrine or theory and must be approached pragmatically against the background of extensive practical military experiences.

From the vantage of an outsider who has labored under the impression that in Central Europe NATO confronted an acute and growing military threat on the part of the Warsaw Pact, the Vienna talks are conducted in a seemingly anomalous atmosphere. No official delegate of any country with whom I talked considered military aggression against the West a likely policy preference of the Soviet leadership. This does not obviate Western concerns about the evidence of an unrelenting buildup of Warsaw Pact military power in the area, consisting in recent years more of armaments modernization than of significant increases in troop strength. But short of a disastrous deterioration of the existing relationship of forces, war is ruled out as a viable option in this region.

In fact, the rationale of the Vienna talks is not so much the avoidance of war as the preservation of peace. Both sides are agreed that the general objective of the negotiations should be to contribute to a more stable relationship and to the strengthening of peace in Europe, without diminishing the security of any party to the negotiations. They also agree that the best way to achieve this objective would be through a modest reduction of massed military forces confronting each other. They do not aim at millennial results, such as the elimination of the confrontation itself. On the contrary, they operate on the premise that the confrontation between adversary systems will continue indefinitely. What they seek to accomplish is to

To allay fears of a surprise attack.

diminish the intensity of the confrontation by relatively small reductions of military forces.

Western proposals, which are expressed in absolute numbers, in effect call for reductions that range from a minimum of 10 percent for NATO ground force manpower to a maximum of 25 percent for Warsaw Pact troops. The Eastern approach, which is by preference couched in percentage terms, calls for equal reductions for both sides ranging from 15 to 17 percent. Thus, even under optimal conditions as set forth by the West, massive military formations numbering some 700,000 ground and approximately 200,000 air force personnel supported by ample armaments would remain in place on each side after the schedule of reductions had been completed.[2] It is doubtful that reductions on such a limited scale would be enough to ensure the elimination of the risk of war. Nevertheless, they could exert a significant stabilizing influence by allaying still further the existing apprehensions on both sides about a surprise attack with little warning; by damping down the competitive upward spiral of armaments and related costs; by enhancing confidence in the prospect of a peaceful resolution of conflicts; and, in the final analysis, by helping to create a climate for increasingly constructive East-West political and economic cooperation.

UNDERLYING ISSUES

The substantial agreement between the two sides concerning the objectives of the talks imparts an air of businesslike practicality and pragmatism to the proceedings in Vienna. The negotiators are preeminently issue-oriented and approach their difficult tasks without being unduly burdened by excessive ideological trappings (although these are not wholly absent in all cases). This has a beneficial effect on the procedural aspects of the talks. Yet it has not gone far enough toward resolving the profound substantive differences that exist between East and West, in regard to their respective interpretations of what precise conditions need to be met to assure a more stable relationship and the strengthening of peace in Europe, and by what means these conditions can best be attained. This constitutes the crux of their disagreement, which they have not been able to overcome in four years of negotiation.

The East essentially seeks to preserve the status quo at lower levels in the East-West force relationship. The premise on which it acts is that this force relationship, as it has become established in Europe since World War II, has in fact helped to preserve the peace for a long period. Maintaining this force relationship would therefore not diminish the security of any party to the negotiations. On the other hand, proportionately lowering the forces confronting each

*West wants an offsided reduction.
WTO wants an equal reduction.*

other (by equal percentage reductions) would help to
bring about a more stable relationship, further
strengthening peace. It is not possible to accuse the
East of seeking additional advantages. It simply seeks
to maintain its superiority in numbers and to legitimize it by gaining the West's formal acceptance.

The West, naturally, objects to what it regards as
the perpetuation of a superior military posture on the
part of the East. Thus, the Western approach aims at
changing the status quo by replacing the existing Eastern superiority in military manpower with what is
called approximate parity and, for good measure, by
also reducing the East's overwhelming preponderance in
numbers of tanks. The West's aims are understandable
and defensible from the point of view of logic and
equity. If implemented, they would indeed tend to
create a more stable relationship and contribute to the
strengthening of peace in Europe. The East, however,
does not see it that way. It claims that NATO's demands for disproportionate or asymmetrical reductions,
in order to arrive at a common or equal ceiling in
military manpower between the two sides, would in effect diminish the security of the Warsaw Pact countries. Although this line of argumentation may seem
self-serving, it is not entirely that. In actuality,
the Warsaw Pact is being asked to give up an advantage,
which might well diminish its sense of security.

The opposing perceptions presented here in capsule
form have informed the agenda of the Vienna negotiations.

POLITICAL CHARACTER OF THE NEGOTIATIONS

It is evident that the talks concern the size,
configuration, and disposition of military forces on
both sides, to determine by how much and in what manner
they should be reduced. Strict military considerations, however, are secondary to political considerations. These are not disarmament negotiations in the
proper sense of the term. What is at stake in Vienna
is the forging of a political agreement in which military force dispositions are the integral component.
The military is seen primarily as an instrument of
political pressure, and the consequences of the existing military confrontation are perceived as predominantly political and psychological, especially in
the impact they have on Western governments and public
opinion. This must be understood if the rationale of
the talks is to be properly assessed, the atmosphere of
the negotiations appreciated, and the relative influence of civilian negotiators and their military advisors evaluated.

Civilian negotiators are in charge of the conduct
of the negotiations, but since the subject matter is
military, they must rely on military intelligence

estimates and on the professional judgment of their
military advisors. This would seem to impart certain
privileges to the military advisors who in a sense act
in a dual capacity--as suppliers of indispensable information and appraisers of the merits of arrangements
arrived at on the basis of this information.

INFLUENCE AND ATTITUDE OF MILITARY ADVISORS

My efforts to determine how much influence the
military advisors actually wield in shaping the content
of negotations were not eminently successful. Civilians on both sides tended to soft-pedal the policy
inputs of their respective military advisors. At the
same time, they were inclined to upgrade the possible
influence of military advisors on the other side,
though a number of them said that on neither side did
the military have excessive influence. Western military representatives with whom I spoke evaded any specific characterization of the part they play in determining NATO policy, but they attributed a dominant role
to their Soviet counterparts in formulating Warsaw Pact
policy. I could neither confirm nor refute their con-
tentions, since I did not speak to any Eastern military
men.

I am not able to form a firm opinion about how
much influence Western military advisors exercise. On
the basis of my discussions with them, I am persuaded
that they are on the whole less enthusiastic than their
civilian counterparts about the enterprise in which
they are engaged, more skeptical about the possibility
of an equitable--let alone favorable--outcome, and far
more suspicious about the motives and objectives of the
adversary.

These advisors profess not to comprehend why the
Soviet Union joined the talks in the first place, if it
were not to gain advantages. They have great difficulty giving any credence to the notion that the Warsaw
Pact might allow the numerical superiority which it
clearly has in the field (in manpower and tanks, if not
in other armaments) to be whittled down through diplomatic negotiations. Looking at things in a narrow
military framework, they see no reason why anyone would
give up a battlefield advantage unless forced to do so.
Moreover, they perceive continuing evidence of aggressive intent in the massed formations of Warsaw Pact
troops and tanks poised across a border that is barely
adequately defended.

From their study of Soviet military doctrine, the
advisors conclude that the USSR is offensively oriented, harnessed as it is to a political ideology with
expansionist aims of global proportions.

It would be farfetched to say that the Western
military advisors distrust the steadfastness of NATO

civilian negotiators, but it is clear that they are apprehensive about what might be given away for the sake
of political compromise. They would favor attaining
parity with the Warsaw Pact, not by paring down the
forces of both sides to equal levels but by building up
NATO forces to match those of the Warsaw Pact.

SUSPICIONS AND THREAT PERCEPTIONS

Suspicions and threat perceptions, of course, are
not the exclusive domain of the Western military. The
Russians, Czechs, Poles, and East Germans look askance
at many internal developments in the Federal Republic
of Germany, while the West Germans distrust the motives
and objectives of the Eastern countries, particularly
Russia. Wartime and other historic experiences are too
vividly etched in the memories of some participants to
be easily obliterated. They are not willing to let
bygones be bygones, to bury the past, and to give each
other sufficient credit for having changed for the
better.

The specter of the Wehrmacht still haunts the
East, which tends to view the Bundeswehr as the direct
descendant of that dread war machine. Nor are the
Eastern representatives convinced that democracy has
become firmly entrenched in the Federal Republic. They
are all too ready to seize on the slightest sign of
internal instability, political polarization, resurgent
revanchism, and authoritarianism to justify their contention that the Federal Republic is not fully trust-
worthy, since it retains the social fabric and economic
structure that spawned Hitler's Reich. A recent case
in point--over which they became quite exercised--was
the wave of terrorism that swept over the Federal
Republic and the severe reaction of the government and
the people to it. The East also feels that the Federal
Republic strives for military hegemony in Western Europe and that this motive has slowed and may block
progress toward the conclusion of an agreement, the
terms of which would substantially curtail the size of
West German military forces.

For their part, the West Germans are very sensitive about any arrangement which in their view would
discriminate against their exercise of sovereign
rights. This includes, of course, the determination of
the size of their military. They act in part on the
basis of historic reminiscences that date from the
Versailles peace treaty after World War I, by which the
victorious Western allies imposed humiliating punitive
restrictions on the Weimar Republic.

In the contemporary context, the West Germans do
not want to be disadvantaged vis-a-vis the Soviet Union
or vis-a-vis their Western allies. They are mindful
that theirs is the most important country on either

Disadvantage of FRG: If lies within reduction area
and therefore will have a maximum limit on its
military while Britain, France and the U.S. will
34   only have to reduce their forces within the
reduction area.

side whose territory lies entirely within the area in
which troop reductions are to take place.   This means
that national force limits agreed on in the compass of
an MBFR agreement would put an absolute ceiling on
their military.   Other countries, East or West, whose
territory lies outside the reduction area would not
have to contend with such strictures.   (These countries
include not only the Soviet Union but also the United
States and Great Britain, who are direct participants
in the talks; Italy, a special participant; and even
France, which is not participating, although it has
troops stationed in the Federal Republic.)   An MBFR
agreement would limit only the forces these countries
maintain in the reduction area.   They would otherwise
be free to determine the size of their military establishment as they saw fit.
     The persistence of very deep-rooted suspicions
among the participants about each other's intentions
may account for a well-nigh obsessive concern which
all delegates expressed over the "contractualization"
of a fancied or real, actual or potential, advantage on
the part of the "other side." At the same time, of
course, preoccupation with contractualization may be
interpreted as a sign of serious intent to reach a
workable and lasting agreement by plugging as many
loopholes as possible that might otherwise tempt the
parties to cheat.
     In defense of their concern over contractualiza-
tion, representatives from both sides set forth quite
sophisticated arguments that helped to explain why they
opposed certain proposals introduced by the other side.
For example, a proposal by the East about non-increase
of ground force manpower (that is, a freeze beginning
immediately and continuing until an agreement on force
reductions is reached) at first glance appears quite
harmless, at least to an innocent observer.   It has not
found favor with the West.   This is largely due to the
fear that accepting it would be tantamount to the
contractualization of existing disparities in force
levels and would undermine the credibility of the
West's insistence on ultimately reaching a common level
of forces on both sides.   Additionally, the West is
leery that a freeze on troops would also imply the
contractualization of existing quantitative ratios in
armaments, in which the East also has a substantial
lead.   This could mean a long-term advantage for the
East.   While the West could not increase the quantity
of its armaments, the East could proceed to modernize
its weapons and thus make inroads on the West's existing qualitative lead, which is a major factor in maintaining an approximate balance.
     The East, in turn, demurs at the implications of
the contractualization of the principle of collectivity
for alliance forces, which is advocated by the West and

Fear of "contractualization";
giving a legal advantage
over to the other side.

eg troop levels: acceptance of
Soviet proposed troop freeze reduces
West's bargaining position for UN
reduction and equity and also implies an
acknowledgment/in of troops

runs counter to the East's preference for national ceilings. The reason for the East's apprehensions is that under the provisions of collectivity the West would safeguard its total troop strength against erosion, in the event that one or another member state unilaterally decided to withdraw a portion of its troops stationed in the reduction area. Should such an eventuality arise, the West would be at liberty to make up for the missing numbers by an increase in the troop strength of another or several other participants.

What concerns the East most is its anticipation that the whole scheme is designed to provide opportunities for an augmentation of West German forces. Warsaw Pact representatives are apprehensive that, if such increases were in fact sanctioned by international treaty, the West German government would find it relatively easy to obtain parliamentary approval for them and could also secure the allocation of appropriate resources. Under present circumstances, the East believes that such attempts would encounter strong political opposition. To buttress its case, the East argues that the collective ceiling formula, which would in fact not rule out increases in troop strength, violates the fundamental principle of troop reductions. This argument is not devoid of logic and plausibility, but it fails to consider what is likely to be politically feasible under any circumstances. The Federal Republic's allies would hardly countenance a major expansion of West German military power. But the Soviet Union and its allies understandably cannot be guided in determining their national security by confident expectations that the Western powers will at all times act sensibly and with regard for Soviet sensitivities. Hence, the Eastern formula calling for national ceilings--which in fact would prohibit any increase in the forces of any participating country from the lowest level attained through treaty agreement.

PROBLEM AREAS

There is no issue within the compass of MBFR that does not represent a problem. Even the area of reduction, somewhat peculiarly identified as Central Europe (since it extends in the West from the Netherlands, Belgium, Luxembourg, and through the Federal Republic of Germany to the German Democratic Republic, Czechoslovakia, and Poland in the East), has not been definitively delimited. NATO has reserved the right to raise the question of the possible inclusion of Hungary, a country that is contiguous with the reduction area and one in which four Soviet divisions are stationed.

The geographic factor in general tends to preoccupy the West, for it feels that the Soviet Union derives unique advantages from its proximity to the

reduction area. A formidable array of troops amount-
ing to upwards of sixty divisions are stationed in
Western Russia, a staging area whence they can be
transferred to the reduction area quickly and perhaps
without timely detection by the West. The reinforcement of NATO troops from the United States is far more
time-consuming and complicated, despite provisions that
have been made and exercises that have been held to
cope with such a contingency. The West has argued that
this unequal condition, attendant upon the forces of
the two superpowers, is one justification for larger
reductions by the Soviet Union. To no avail. The East
has countered that, for one thing, troops withdrawn
from the reduction area would be demobilized. For another, the reintroduction of old troops or introduction
of new ones above the authorized limit would constitute
a violation of any treaty or agreement entered into by
the Soviet Union. That would entail untoward consequences which would neither be consistent with the
purpose of force reductions in Central Europe nor serve
Soviet interests. As to the alleged advantage of the
Soviet Union's geographic location, the East has argued
that it is a disadvantage as well. Western Russia is
vulnerable both to ground attack and exposure to a
variety of nuclear weapons stored in Western Europe,
whereas the United States continues to enjoy immunity
from Soviet attack by any but strategic arms.
     Associated measures that could encompass a number
of things (such as prior notification of troop movements in the area, limitations on the scope of maneuvers, verification, and inspection) are obviously important adjuncts of any comprehensive agreement to be
concluded. There is little evidence that a meeting of
minds has been achieved about any of the component
elements of "associated measures."
     Similarly, the security of flank countries in the
North (Norway, Denmark) and in the South (Italy, Turkey, Greece, Bulgaria, Hungary, and Romania) has not
been extensively deliberated upon. Both areas represent sensitive pressure points. As much calamity could
result from military aggression there as on the central
front. While the situation on the Southern flank is
not ominous from the Western point of view since NATO
forces are in preponderance there, the opposite is true
in the North, where the Soviet Union maintains formidable naval concentrations.
     There are four paramount issues which have re-
ceived more attention than others and have been more
arduously debated among the participants throughout
four years of negotiations:

     1. The actual facts as regards the starting
        point for computing manpower reductions
        (discussed below under the heading "data")

2. The scope and methods of reduction; in
    other words, who reduces, what, how (in
    relation to other countries), and when
    (discussed below under the heading "mo-
    dalities")
3. The limitations on residual force levels
    after reduction
4. The problem of armaments reductions

DATA

The dispute over the number of ground forces the
Warsaw Pact maintains in the reduction area has been
the central contentious issue of the negotiations since
their inception. Briefly, in 1973 the West claimed
that the East had about 150,000 more men in the field
than had NATO (925,000 Warsaw Pact versus 777,000
NATO). The East originally did not challenge Western
figures, although it did not explicitly acknowledge
their accuracy. Indirectly, however, Eastern statements both in Vienna and elsewhere seemed to confirm
Western claims, because the Eastern side propounded a
doctrine of military superiority designed to safeguard the peace in Europe. Moreover, Eastern spokesmen
proclaimed that by virtue of the existing correlation
of forces (that is, Eastern military superiority in the
center of Europe along the East-West dividing line) the
peace had in fact been safeguarded for over a quarter
of a century.

Prodded by the West to enter into a discussion of
data pertaining to manpower, the East (sometime in the
winter of 1975) began to shift its position, asserting
that an approximate parity in forces prevailed. Dis-
satisfied with this attempt to circumvent the question,
the West continued pressure on the East to table pertinent information. On June 10, 1976, the East did in
fact table figures, which showed a total of 987,000
troops: 805,000 ground forces and the rest air force.
Significant as this move was, given deeply ingrained
Soviet insistence on secrecy of military information of
any kind, and important as it was as a signal of Soviet
responsiveness to Western insistence, the tabled figures fell far below the Western estimates of Warsaw
Pact forces in the area. The move actually compounded
the problem because the East was now officially on the
public record with a set of figures from which it could
not easily depart.

The West subsequently asked for a detailed breakdown of these figures in order to arrive at a determination of the roots of the existing discrepancy between
its intelligence estimates and the Soviet data. After
more than a year of fruitless discussion, the East
showed readiness to break down its figures into national components. But the West rejected this idea

essentially on the unstated ground that exchanging national data could be interpreted by the East as a precedent that might legitimize the concept of "national ceilings." Instead, the West continued to demand a breakdown of Warsaw Pact figures into groups corresponding to major military formations.

Two questions may be asked. Why the attachment to men as the crucial units of reduction and why the hue and cry over an alleged Eastern superiority of roughly 150,000 men? Answers are not easily forthcoming and are not fully convincing. Basically, in the view of Western military experts, the complexity of truly equitable mutual reductions of military forces with all their fighting gear is so great that the issues to be delt with could not be satisfactorily resolved. Standards of equivalence defy the imagination, for qualitative judgments have to be made and there is no generally accepted doctrine. In the absence of such standards and doctrine it would be futile to try for what is a truly comprehensive reduction of military forces. Military manpower should thus be the essential measure. This is antithetical to the comprehensive global approach to reduction advocated by the Warsaw Pact on the premise that equivalence in combat units should be sought.

Qualitative disparities exist in regard to equipment and men as well. One can legitimately question the worth of one fighting man as compared with that of another. But it is inconceivable that formal discussions could be conducted with explicit reference to any qualitative difference that might exist between the fighting capacity, the level of training, or the degree of motivation of troops from different countries. Therefore, the essential equivalence of men across the board has to be accepted for purposes of discussion. A further practical argument is that there is at least a crude relationship between numbers of men and combat capability, for it is men who must drive tanks, fire guns, launch missiles, and so forth. This straightforward quantitative approach to manpower could give rise to apprehensions on the part of Warsaw Pact representatives. Strict numerical parity would put a high premium on the quality of armaments, and this would tilt the balance in favor of the West.

What about the real significance of the Warsaw Pact's superiority in manpower? At the given force levels on both sides, a lead of some 150,000 men represents about 15 percent of the Warsaw Pact forces by Western estimates and nearly 20 percent by Eastern estimates. Is such a margin of superiority of decisive importance in strict military terms, giving the Warsaw Pact an overwhelming advantage for a standing start attack that would assure quick and certain victory? The answer is likely to be no. Moreover, the possibility does exist that the gap between NATO and Warsaw Pact ground force manpower may in fact be somewhat smaller than 150,000. Not that Western intelligence services who supplied the gross figures necessarily engaged in a deliberate overestimation of Warsaw Pact forces. In all likelihood, they were scrupulously accurate in putting forth their estimates; and in all probability, the intelligence capability of the West is good enough to reduce margins of error to a few percentage points. But a few percentage points in Western estimates, say anywhere from three to five, would account for some 27,000 to 45,000 men; and it is reasonable to assume that if Western intelligence erred, it erred on the high rather than the low side. Then, too, there is the unanswered question of how Western intelligence arrived at its figures. Without going into possible methods of computation, one can suggest that the size of Eastern military forces may be inflated if it included soldiers in uniform, who in the Warsaw Pact armies perform tasks that are usually assigned to civilians in the West. If an equivalent contingent of civilians working for the military were included in the overall total of NATO forces, the figures might be closer to approximate parity. For example, according to a White Paper issued by the Federal German minister of defense, as of November 1, 1973, "about 120,000 civilians, mostly Germans [were] employed in support of . . . allied forces [stationed on the territory of the Federal Republic of Germany]. Through their work . . . they, too, contribute to the mission of the alliance and thus to security."[3] Finally, it is possible that certain units counted as air force components in the West were inadvertently charged against ground force units in the East.

Whatever the case may be, the two sides are having great difficulties in reconciling their differences. According to information released by Eastern sources, the ratio between ground forces is 805,000 for the Warsaw Pact to 791,000 for NATO. This would indeed represent approximate parity. The Eastern total for NATO forces includes some 60,000 French soldiers. While France is not participating in the talks, it has troops stationed in the Federal Republic of Germany and has declared that it will fight on the side of NATO, should hostilities break out.[4] But despite occasional Eastern remarks to the contrary, NATO totals are not in serious dispute. They correspond to published accounts in Western parliamentary proceedings and budgets and are corroborated by Western spokesmen in Vienna, who place the current level of NATO forces at "somewhat in excess" of the standard figure of 777,000 used since the inception of the talks. It is the Warsaw Pact total that is being questioned. Judging by commentaries in Soviet and East European newspapers,

Western estimates now put the number of Warsaw Pact ground forces in the neighborhood of 950,000. In terms of reduction to a common ceiling of 700,000, which the West postulates "illustratively" rather than in the form of an official proposal, Warsaw Pact troop strength would have to be reduced by 250,000 as compared with approximately 91,000 NATO troops.

Attempts to clarify the manpower picture and its implications from publicly available data are frustrating and unsatisfactory, and they have limited validity because of the contested accuracy of the data base. Yet I have attempted to tabulate figures to illustrate a possible range of comparisons between NATO and Warsaw Pact forces and to suggest the existence of interesting force relationships, if comparisons are made on a more restricted basis than areawide manpower totals.

I used three sets of figures published in the 1977-78 edition of The Military Balance, an annual tome of the London-based International Institute for Strategic Studies (IISS): total Soviet ground forces, numbers and types of divisions the Soviet Union maintains in the three East European countries in the reduction area, and estimated full divisional strengths. By comparing two sets of figures in different combinations, I obtained widely divergent subtotals for Soviet troop strength in the respective countries and also two different areawide totals. Dividing overall areawide manpower with numbers of known divisions in the region gives one set of subtotals per country: 352,000 in the German Democratic Republic, 88,000 in Czechoslovakia, 35,000 in Poland. Multiplying numbers of divisions by the estimated number of men at full divisional strength gives another set of country subtotals: 237,000 in the German Democratic Republic, 60,000 in Czechoslovakia, 22,000 in Poland. When added, these subtotals give a total of only 319,000, or much less than the overall Soviet troop strength of 460,000-475,000 most commonly quoted. One reason for this discrepancy may be that not all troops are contained in divisional formations, and for that reason alone, the lower estimate of Soviet manpower is highly suspect.

The calculations in the preceding paragraph and the numerical comparisons attempted in the ensuing paragraphs are not meant to contest the accuracy of Western data, nor the Western contention that an imbalance exists in the force levels of the two alliances in favor of the Warsaw Pact. Rather, I seek to illustrate a variety of ways in which force comparisons can be made and the conclusions one can draw from them. For purposes of uniformity, Soviet troop strength is calculated at the estimated maximum of 475,000 in each instance.

Clearly, the disparity between U.S. and Soviet forces is considerable: 190,000 to 475,000 for a ratio of two to five. The proportion of West German troops to Soviet forces, however, is less one-sided: 345,000 to 475,000 or a little better than two to three. The combined forces of the United States and the Federal Republic of Germany outnumber those of the Soviet Union by 535,000 to 475,000. As for the Federal Republic vis-a-vis its two Eastern neighbors, the German Democratic Republic and Czechoslovakia, respective troop strengths are one-sidedly in favor of the Federal Republic (345,000 to 105,000 East German and 135,000 Czechoslovak troops). The Federal Republic outnumbers the combined troop strength of its two neighbors by a margin of approximately seven to four.

Total NATO troop strength in the Federal Republic of Germany (including French troops) outnumbers total Warsaw Pact troop concentrations in the German Democratic Republic and Czechoslovakia by a narrow margin (731,000 to 715,000). The margin of NATO superiority across the most acute single frontier (between the Federal Republic and the German Democratic Republic, which is some 870 miles in length) is much greater (731,000 to 457,000). The last of the comparisons between the two countries is strongly artificial. NATO troops are stationed throughout the territory of the Federal Republic. Many face the Czechoslovak border. It is an open question how many could be appropriately included in a pairing with Soviet and East German troops along the border between the two German states.

I could not argue convincingly that the troops stationed in Poland, a country in the area of reduction, should be left out of consideration when comparing East-West forces in the context of MBFR. Nor is it my purpose to do so. I am not sure, however, how justified it is to expect that all Polish forces, numbering some 220,000 ground troops, would be engaged in a Warsaw Pact assault on the West. I find it inconceivable that in the event of war Poland could be stripped of all national military forces. The number of Soviet troops in Poland does not exceed 35,000. Even if all were transferred to the "front," they would not significantly augment Warsaw Pact military manpower. The question I have, however, is whether the Soviet Union would be inclined to remove its entire garrison from Poland.

To be sure, there are massed forces in Western Russia in the vicinity of the Soviet-Polish border. These could be called upon to reinforce the Soviet garrison in Poland or to replace it. And masses of Soviet troops could be easily transported westward across Poland and the German Democratic Republic--a distance of some 400 miles. Compared with the distance over which U.S. troops would need to be airlifted to Western Europe, 400 miles is negligible. The Soviet Union thus enjoys a distinct advantage. The West's preoccupation with the implications of the geographic factor appears to have substance. Yet anyone who has travelled by auto or rail in this part of Europe knows that it takes some twelve to fifteen hours to traverse Poland and the German Democratic Republic in an East-West direction (exclusive of any delays one may encounter on the border and elsewhere). How long would it take to stage a major transfer of troops along the existing transportion routes? Would such a transfer escape detection? Finally, in a comparison of numbers, should trained reserves be excluded from consideration?

The data dispute is not likely to be susceptible to a mutually satisfactory resolution in military terms. But in essence the dispute has more political and psychological connotations than strictly military ones.

Both sides have staked out firm claims on numbers. How can they relent without a disastrous loss of face and attendant loss of credibility? Can the West admit that its intelligence estimates were grossly incorrect? Or, still worse, can it admit that it knowingly inflated Warsaw Pact troop strength for political purposes? Similarly, can the East publicly corroborate the accuracy of the figures presented by the West, which it has steadfastly repudiated?

MODALITIES

The question of data pervades the entire fabric of negotiations. It is a crucial aspect of the hotly disputed issue of the modalities of reduction, for it is clearly not a matter of indifference to anyone which country's troops are reduced, in what numbers, and in what proportion to the troops withdrawn by other countries. The stratagems and maneuvers of the two sides aim chiefly at whittling down the military force of the respective chief adversaries: the Soviet Union in the East and the Federal Republic of Germany (not the United States) in the West. Both sides have introduced ingenious proposals which have hardly managed to disguise the real intent behind them.

The NATO proposal essentially calls for a two-phase reduction, the major (first-phase) feature to consist of the withdrawal of 29,000 American troops and a Soviet tank army consisting of 68,000 men (including their equipment and 1,700 tanks). Other countries would reduce only in the second phase, at an unspecified time and in amounts to be defined later.

On the face of it, this is a thoroughly lopsided, asymmetrical reduction scheme and has been so denounced by the Warsaw Pact. The underlying premise of this

43

scheme is that the superpowers must reduce first, in
significant numbers and in proportion to their respective troop strength. It will be noted that 29,000 is
almost exactly 15 percent of the total number of U.S.
troops in West Germany, and 68,000 is just about an
identical percentage of 460,000, the approximate average estimate of Soviet troop strength in the area of
reduction. The West might as well define its proposal
for reductions in percentages. That it refrains from
doing so is undoubtedly due to its reluctance to commit
itself to percentages for any purpose. It fears le-
gitimizing the East's formula for troop reductions
which is always set forth in percentage terms and
which, if adopted, would redound strongly in NATO's
disfavor.

But apart from the reasons for using absolute numbers as against percentages, the West's proposal does
have far-reaching qualitative connotations. The United
States would withdraw troops at random, essentially on
an individual or small unit basis which would constitute a moderate thinning of its ranks. The Soviet
Union, in turn, would be obligated to withdraw a major
combat force. Calculations made by Robert L. Fischer,
a staff member of the U.S. Arms Control and Disarmament
Agency (ACDA), show convincingly that the implementation of this proposal would reduce Soviet forces by
approximately 50,000 combat personnel, as compared with
about 14,000 U.S. combat personnel. In terms of the
"size of a massed Warsaw Pact breakthrough force using
only peacetime forces," the reduction would mean a drop
of some 20 percent, as compared with a drop of only
4 percent in commensurate NATO corps strength.[5]

In the West's frame of reference, an asymmetrical
reduction of this magnitude is fully justified. It
would bring the combat capabilities of the two sides
nearer to parity and would significantly improve NATO's
military position. The Warsaw Pact reaction is not
difficult to imagine. For one thing, objections were
raised to the bilateral aspects of the reduction plan.
The pairing of the United States and the Soviet Union
within the geographic confines of the area under discussion did not seem equitable, especially since nothing was said at all about the disposition to be made of
345,000 Bundeswehr soldiers. The lack of specificity
concerning the timing of a second, follow-on phase of
reductions and the obligations of other NATO countries
to reduce their forces on that occasion was also
troubling to the Warsaw Pact countries. They had no
assurance that a second phase would in fact take place.
That the vagueness of the West's second-phase proposal
also exempted the German Democratic Republic, Poland,
and Czechoslovakia from making firm reduction commitments was of little consequence to the Warsaw Pact.
These countries would just as soon reduce their

military forces in order to reallocate much needed
resources to the civilian economy.

Identical percentage reductions as advocated by
the East give the appearance of equality and would in
fact correspond to parity, if forces of the same magnitude were being reduced. But in actuality, reductions
carried out in this manner would not obliterate the
proportional disparity of force levels which the West
claims exists, although they would reduce the gap between NATO and Warsaw Pact forces in absolute numbers.
There might be a certain value in that alone, but
obviously it is not enough to satisfy NATO.

For example, a 15 percent across-the-board reduction from present force levels (assuming a starting
number of 791,000 for NATO and 950,000 for the Warsaw
Pact) would give the following end results: NATO reduction total would equal 118,650 as compared with
142,500 for the Warsaw Pact; residual force levels
would be 672,350 for NATO and 807,500 for the Warsaw
Pact; and the difference between them would be 135,150,
instead of the starting disparity of 159,000.

The Warsaw Pact scheme of 15 percent reductions
would have the undesirable effect of cutting more
deeply into NATO manpower and less deeply into the
manpower of the Eastern forces than would be the case
under the fixed ceiling scheme favored by the West.
But the most insidious effect, from the Western point
of view, would be the imposition of permanent national
ceilings on the military forces in the area of reduction. While all countries would be affected, the Federal Republic of Germany would feel the impact of these
restrictions most keenly.

To move discussion about modalities off dead center, the Warsaw Pact agreed in February 1976 to a two-
phase reduction, separating the superpowers from the
remaining countries by reducing their forces before the
others. This was done only with the proviso that the
entire process of reduction be agreed on in conjunction
with first-phase reductions, and that all countries
obligate themselves to a fixed scope of reductions
during the second phase. Western representatives have
derided this concession as meaningless. While it is
not that (for it reflects at least a gesture in the
place of utterly rigid rejection), its accommodating of
the West is more apparent than real. A similar Western
gesture not to delay the beginning of the second phase
of reductions unreasonably, and perhaps even to set a
date for it upon Soviet agreement to the terms of
NATO's first-phase reduction, failed to satisfy the
expectation of the Warsaw Pact.

LIMITATIONS ON RESIDUAL FORCE LEVELS

Limiting residual force levels after reduction is,
in a sense, the most important task of MBFR. For

regardless of the starting point of reductions and the methods of implementing them, it is the end result with which NATO and Warsaw Pact countries will have to contend over the long run. Obviously, neither side can accept an outcome it considers unfavorable. Each side has set forth a model that satisfies its perceptions of adequate security, but not necessarily those of the other side.

The Eastern model is consistent with the aim of perpetuating the proportional numerical superiority which the Warsaw Pact gradually built up and which was in place at the start of the negotiations. As stated above, it also has the effect of placing severe, absolute restraints on the military power of the seven countries whose territory is in the reduction area (the Federal Republic of Germany, Belgium, the Netherlands, and Luxembourg in the West and the German Democratic Republic, Poland, and Czechoslovakia in the East). Under an agreement signed on these terms, there would be a permanent freeze on the size of their entire military establishment. In contrast, the other participating countries (the United States, Great Britain, and Canada in the West and the USSR in the East) whose territory lies outside the confines of the reduction area would be privileged in that restrictions would affect only the forces they may keep in the reduction area. The inequity of these provisions is self-evident. They would keep a lid on the military potential of the most vulnerable NATO power which also has the largest number of ground forces--the Federal Republic of Germany-- without similarly restricting the dominant Warsaw Pact power. The integrity of NATO defenses would be further jeopardized since there would be no way of compensating for any voluntary unilateral force reduction which one or another participating country might want to undertake, subsequent to an MBFR agreement.

The Western model for residual force levels would, of course, safeguard NATO from such untoward consequences. For one thing, it would create true numerical parity between the forces of the two alliance systems. For another, it would provide a flexible, self-correcting mechanism for maintaining the maximum allowable collective manpower ceiling, regardless of any unilateral force reduction on the part of a member of the alliance. Most important, it would avoid the codification of an odious principle--limiting the national sovereignty of member states through international agreement. As noted earlier, this is of particular significance for the Federal Republic of Germany, not only from a strictly military point of view but also for political and psychological reasons.

The Western model takes into account all components bearing on the integrity of NATO defenses and the cohesiveness of the alliance, without increasing the real or potential threat to the Warsaw Pact. But this

does not guarantee that the East will be willing to
abandon its stubbornly held preferences.

THE PROBLEM OF ARMAMENTS REDUCTIONS

No subject is more important yet less well understood outside the circle of negotiators in Vienna (and
perhaps NATO headquarters in Brussels and the Warsaw
Pact high command in Moscow) than the problem of armaments reductions. One reason for this is that almost
nothing has been written about it. Any discussions the
two sides may have had about the reduction of armaments
have been shrouded in still greater silence than other
phases of MBFR. The starting positions of the two
sides were, once again, widely divergent. The East
proposed an integrated approach to reductions that
would include designated combat units with all their
men and equipment; the West favored a disaggregated
approach that separates manpower reduction from armaments reduction.

The Western position, however, as we have seen has
not been fully consistent. The original 1973 NATO
proposal for first-phase reductions affecting the
United States and the USSR stipulated the withdrawal of
a Soviet tank army, lock, stock, and barrel. As an
inducement to the Warsaw Pact to accept these terms, in
December 1975, the United States made a "one-time"
offer to trade off the reduction of specified numbers
of American nuclear warheads and delivery vehicles for
the withdrawal of the Soviet tank army.[6] In the fall
of 1977, NATO was reported considering modifying its
1973 proposal. The new terms would permit the Soviet
Union to withdraw a specified number of units and tanks
from the entire reduction area.

The Warsaw Pact's reaction to the 1973 proposal
was understandably cool. The 1975 U.S. offer elicited
a great deal of Eastern condemnation in public, but it
was in fact countered within the confines of the negotiations by a counterproposal calling for the withdrawal by both sides of equal numbers of precisely
defined, sophisticated armaments. That is where matters appear to rest for the time being.[7]

It is not easy to unravel the facts about the
armaments picture. The Warsaw Pact appears to have an
overwhelming superiority in tanks, far in excess of its
numerial superiority in men. According to Western
figures, the Warsaw Pact disposes of more than 16,000
tanks while NATO has about 6,500. Thus, the East has
an absolute advantage of roughly 9,500 (or a ratio of
about two-and-a-half to one). These figures have not
been publicly disputed. In the realm of battlefield
nuclear weapons, in turn, the United States is reputed
to have a better than two-to-one edge over the Soviet
Union. Clearly, the West is primarily concerned over

tanks and the East over nuclear weapons. It is difficult to see, however, to what degree NATO's plight
would be relieved by the withdrawal of 1,500 to 1,700
Soviet tanks, and how much the Warsaw Pact's security
would be enhanced by the withdrawal of 1,000 U.S.
nuclear warheads from an arsenal of some 7,500.

STATUS OF TALKS

Notwithstanding the plethora of vicissitudes that
beset MBFR, the Vienna negotiations show no sign of
faltering. They are grinding ahead laboriously for, as
many representatives told me, the talks are "doomed to
succeed." None of the participants would dare to
withdraw, for fear of precipitating widespread adverse
repercussions. Even an adjournment sine die is difficult to envisage. The mere suggestion of a somewhat
longer than usual break elicits alarmed inquiries from
newsmen. Only in the event of a reversal to a cold war
atmosphere would either side consider it politic to
terminate its participation in the talks. Even without
success, they have become a firmly imbedded symbol in
Europe of an attempt to settle dangerous military affairs in a political context around the negotiating
table.
The absence of visible progress to date is not a
true reflection of what has been accomplished. The
delegates in Vienna have deliberately shunned the lime-
light. They tend to obscure from view rather than
illumine for public edification what transpires in
their discussions. The talks are confidential, and
with only a few minor exceptions, both sides have
scrupulously observed the principle of confidentiality.
As a result, the negotiations have a very low visi-
bility. Many people, especially in the United States,
are unaware of their existence.
Press conferences are infrequent, although a
ritual of public statements by both sides at the end of
each negotiating round has become firmly entrenched, as
well as an opening-of-round press statement issued by
the East. (A round is a period of roughly three
months, followed by a pause of about a month, except
for a longer summer break.) But these occasions serve
both sides to display their prowess in the art of dis-
simulation. Unless one is privy to the minutiae of
interaction behind closed doors and extremely well-
versed in the esoteric vocabulary the negotiators have
developed among themselves, the cryptic remarks of the
speakers are impossible to decipher.
In all probability, there has been a certain
amount of foot-dragging by both sides. But other factors also contribute to the excruciatingly slow pace of
the negotiations. The imperatives of alliance diplomacy, especially on the Western side, do not exactly

favor speedy decision making. It is not an expeditious undertaking to push an initiative through the policy machinery of twelve capitals, NATO headquarters, and the local (Vienna) NATO ad hoc group. Nor has the Warsaw Pact, which may not experience identical problems of alliance diplomacy, distinguished itself by the alacrity with which it has responded to Western proposals and the speed with which it has generated new initiatives of its own. The policy process in Moscow is reputed to be very sluggish. Delays have also been engendered by the vagaries of American domestic politics in recent years, including the shock of Watergate and the startling new departures of the Carter administration. The impulses emanating from Washington have not always been clear and consistent. The bewilderment of the Soviet leadership at the unpredictability of American policy is said to have caused the Warsaw Pact to mark time for inordinately long periods.

What has been accomplished is the clarification of respective positions and the identification and recognition of problems, which were not automatically obvious--even to the negotiators--at the outset of the talks. New techniques of alliance diplomacy have also been perfected.

At this juncture in the talks, the West appears to have a positional advantage. The momentum is with it. NATO is making demands on the Warsaw Pact and is setting the terms of discussion, not vice versa. What avail this will have in the long run remains to be seen. The East has more room for maneuver than NATO ever had, and it is, of course, very adept at dilatory tactics in protracted diplomatic encounters. In Vienna, the West seems to be matching the East in patience, perseverance, and craftiness. NATO's present negotiating posture is clearly stronger than, say, at the inception of the talks. Eastern negotiators ruefully admitted as much to me.

In 1973, the Western alliance was in disarray over the consequences of the OPEC oil embargo. The motivations of the United States in promoting force reduction talks were also suspect because of the emphasis given by the American government to the improvement of bilateral relations with the Soviet Union. Moreover, strong congressional pressure was in evidence for unilateral troop withdrawal from Europe. A contemporary objective of MBFR was, in effect, to stave off this congressional pressure, but it was widely believed in Europe that the Nixon administration could not hold the line for very long. The question was not whether but how soon sizable numbers of American troops would have to be withdrawn. In turn, European members of NATO, were experiencing budgetary difficulties in maintaining, let alone expanding, their military establishments, and several countries contemplated unilateral cuts in their forces. These symptoms are not in evidence at present to the same degree. Congressional pressure for troop withdrawal has abated (largely as a consequence of the fall of South Vietnam to the Communists), the budgetary picture of NATO countries has somewhat brightened, and the bloom has long since been off Soviet-American detente. Divisive trends in the alliance have given way to greater cohesion, certainly in Vienna, and doubts about the ability of the United States to stay the course have been substantially dissipated.[8]

FUTURE PROSPECTS

Despite the relatively advantageous position of the West and the muted hope of some Western delegates that the talks will eventually succeed, the rigidity of both sides may preclude the conclusion of a mutually satisfactory accord on troop reductions in Central Europe. From what I have seen in Vienna, I would judge that workable compromises should not be beyond reach within the context of the negotiations. For it seems to me that MBFR as originally conceptualized is an outstanding example of antagonistic cooperation between East and West. It consists essentially of an exploration of ways to cooperate for the achievement of mutually compatible objectives, without giving up the fundamental tenets of rivalry. And MBFR presents an unexcelled opportunity to demonstrate the viability of this sort of relationship, without either succumbing to the extremes of truly cooperative cooperation or the rejection of all cooperation as futile because of the persistence of an elemental antagonism. There are ways in which balances could be obtained and compromises struck, even by preserving reciprocal advantages (if these cannot be overcome). There are large numbers of asymmetrical relationships within MBFR which probably cannot be eliminated or rectified, but they could be paired off so that they essentially balance each other.
It is clear that the sensitivities of the Federal Republic must be respected; but West Germany ultimately will have to reconcile itself to some infringement of its sovereignty, if a meaningful agreement is to be signed. It is important, of course, that limitations on the freedom of decision of the West Germans should not be excessive and that their country should derive commensurate gains in the form of increased security. The Warsaw Pact should not be so blind as to attempt to impose harsh constraints on the defense capacity of the Federal Republic. Attempts to this effect would assuredly not be acceptable to NATO, and they also might be counterproductive in other ways. At some future time, in a political crisis, they might help to revive and feed precisely those revanchist, nationalist

tendencies which the Eastern countries suspect are
still harbored in the psyche of the West German population. The most effective way to encourage continuing
adherence to democracy in the Federal Republic is to
take the political changes that have occurred since the
end of World War II at face value and to promote their
consolidation in a generally tranquil international environment.

To foster confidence among the Western powers, the
Soviet Union should give tangible demonstrations of a
constructive approach to MBFR. For example, the apprehensions of Western powers about the advantages that
geography bestows on the Soviet Union may be somewhat
exaggerated (for one thing, the logistics of supply and
reinforcement of troops even 400-500 miles distant are
not quite as simple as the West makes them out to be).
The Soviet Union, however, would do well to acknowledge
that these fears are genuine. To demonstrate good
faith and allay these fears, the USSR could agree to
place some sort of limitation on the deployment and
movement of troops in Western Russia.

With respect to data, in turn, the West might
consider relenting from its persistent effort to extract from the East further revealing admissions about
its actual troop strength. It is likely that the
figure of 805,000 ground troops tabled by the Warsaw
Pact does not really correspond to the actual number of
men the Warsaw Pact has in military formations in the
reduction area. But it may be a reasonably accurate
extrapolation that corresponds to the deletion from the
total of such uniformed personnel as the East believes
are performing duties which are performed by civilians
for the military in the West. If that were the case,
two somewhat different purposes would be served. Information about Warsaw Pact force structure would be
effectively obscured (which would probably meet the
stringent security requirements of the Soviet military); yet an opportunity would be created for some
upward adjustment of the tabled figure, without loss of
face, on the basis of further clarification of how to
identify identical military formations. That would
narrow the gap between NATO and Warsaw Pact estimates
of Eastern manpower and open the way to a compromise.[9] The West might discover that reductions to an
agreed limit can be carried out without knowing exactly
at what level they started. It is more important to be
able to verify reliably that the agreed-on residual
force levels have been attained and to monitor that
both sides scrupulously observe these limits. The
Soviet Union may not irrevocably oppose verification
and inspection procedures affecting Warsaw Pact troops
outside the territory of the USSR. The question is
whether the Federal Republic of Germany would welcome
the reciprocal verification and inspection of NATO
troops stationed on its territory.

With respect to the modalities of reduction, the outlines of a compromise have become visible. Reduction should proceed in phases, but there should be adequate guarantees against an undue delay between phase one and phase two (which the Warsaw Pact claims to fear). In addition, ironclad commitments should be made that in phase two all countries will in fact reduce in proportion to the number of troops they have in the field.[10] As for residual force levels, the Soviet Union simply must accept the principle of a common ceiling for both sides. The Warsaw Pact reductions would not be credible if they did not create verifiable quantitative parity.[11]

The Soviet Union must also adhere to the principle of collectivity advocated by the West for it is sound, quite apart from being solicitous of West German sensitivities.[12] To make collectivitiy more acceptable to the Warsaw Pact, judicious modifications in its definition might be considered. For example, it should be possible to stipulate that within the framework of collectivity the military forces of neither side should be lopsidedly dominated by the troops of a single country. Thus, a subceiling of perhaps 45 to 50 percent of the total agreed-on number of ground forces could be stipulated as the maximum allowable limit on the troops of any member state of an alliance in the reduction area. This should satisfy the legitimate security concerns of the West Germans without at the same time alarming the Russians, who would have assurances that their worst fears concerning the national force composition of NATO would not come true.[13]

The conclusion of an agreement in Vienna is not solely predicated on the resolution of problems intrinsic to MBFR. Other current international developments significantly impinge on the Vienna negotiations and overshadow them.

MBFR AND OTHER INTERNATIONAL NEGOTIATIONS

The agenda of the Conference on Security and Cooperation in Europe (CSCE) partly overlaps with that of MBFR, although in the West these two international forums were originally perceived as complementary, rather than redundant. At the CSCE follow-up review conference in Belgrade, the Soviet Union appears to be engaged in an effort to gain acceptance in a wider forum and under less stringent conditions for what are essentially "associated measures" in the context of MBFR. It has introduced a plan for limiting the scope of military maneuvers "to 50,000-60,000 troops." This is not inconsistent with the purview of CSCE. Provisions about military measures were included in the Helsinki (CSCE) agreement signed by the thirty-five participants in August 1975. If adopted, the current

plan would apply to all of Europe, and it might even
have a beneficial impact on MBFR.[14]

It is difficult to ascertain what the relationship
between MBFR and the SALT process is and what effect
progress, stagnation, or retrogression in the strategic
arms limitation talks may have on the future of MBFR.
Most delegates in Vienna deny any integral connection
between the two sets of negotiations or a dependency
relationship on the part of MBFR. Nevertheless, they
seem to believe that a satisfactory settlement of outstanding issues in SALT II would have to precede any
breakthrough in MBFR. Chancellor Helmut Schmidt of the
Federal Republic noted somewhat belatedly (in October
1977) that SALT codifies parity between the strategic
systems of the United States and the Soviet Union. As
he put it, the net effect is one of "neutralizing"
these weapons, decreasing the likelihood that the
United States would resort to their use if war were to
break out in Central Europe. He was articulating concerns that SALT II would invalidate the premise on
which the security of Western Europe has long rested,
namely, that U.S. strategic nuclear superiority effectively balanced the numerical superiority of the Warsaw
Pact forces on the ground and thus deterred aggression.[15]

In the absence of a foolproof American strategic
deterrent, the proliferation of "grey area" nuclear
weapons affecting the Central European region becomes
an issue of grave concern that transcends the framework
of MBFR. The terms of reference on which the two sides
agreed in the 1973 preparatory talks excluded the extension of the MBFR framework to cover nuclear weapons.
But even if such an extension were not precluded, the
Vienna negotiations could not cope with intricate new
problems. A separate set of negotiations dealing exclusively with "grey area" problems would seem in order. In such circumstances, the MBFR talks would be
relegated to a position of even lesser importance than
they now have. Still worse, in the view of some observers, the impact of the unrelenting forward march of
weapons technology on the military environment in Central Europe threatens to nullify the assumptions about
conventional forces that underlie MBFR and to rob the
Vienna talks of any relevance.

NOTES

1. The West continues to refer to Mutual and Balanced Force Reductions, although in the 1973 preparatory talks the East rejected the term "balanced" on
the grounds that it connoted asymmetrical reductions,
which the Warsaw Pact rejects in principle.

2. These numbers have since received official
sanction as the common ceiling of residual force levels
on both sides after reduction has taken place.
3. Federal minister of defense, White Paper, 1973-
1974: The Security of the Federal Republic of Germany
and the Development of the Federal Armed Forces (Bonn,
1974), 20.
4. The presence of French troops creates an anomalous situation. Both sides include them in counting
NATO total troop strength. Yet France is not a party
to the negotiations, and it presumably would not feel
itself bound by the terms of an agreement reached in
Vienna. NATO is prepared to absorb French troops in
its residual force levels after reduction, although
this is never stated publicly. Interesting problems
could arise if France chose to substantially reduce its
forces or to remove them altogether. The deficit in
NATO total troop strength would be extremely difficult
to make up. Problems of a different order would arise
if France decided to increase the number of its troops
stationed on the territory of the Federal Republic of
Germany, thereby raising the NATO total over the
agreed-on common ceiling.
5. Robert L. Fischer, Defending the Central Front:
the Balance of Forces, Adelphi Papers, no. 127 (London:
International Institute for Strategic Studies, Fall
1976).
6. The NATO offer was made on a one-time, conditional basis and was to be rescinded if it did not lead
to a first-phase agreement. Known under the designation of "option 3," it proposed the withdrawal of
1,000 nuclear warheads, 54 nuclear capable Phantom
bombers, and 36 Pershing I missile launchers, in addition to 29,000 U.S. soldiers.
7. As stated, the Soviet Union was not responsive
to "option 3." It did, however, indicate interest in
trading off a number of its aircraft (fighter planes)
and land-based nuclear launchers for the U.S. systems.
In this manner, the negotiations would have been ex-
tended to cover the air forces and nuclear systems of
the two sides, which the Soviet Union had favored from
the outset. The West was not amenable to this sort of
quid pro quo, for it insisted on limiting the talks to
the reduction of ground forces. The trade-off between
U.S. nuclear systems and Soviet tanks was never formal-
ized, and "option 3" was ultimately withdrawn. Nevertheless, the Soviet Union did remove 1,000 tanks from
the German Democratic Republic in a voluntary unilateral action (see note 9 below) and the United States
removed 1,000 nuclear warheads in a similar manner,
outside the MBFR framework.
8. The ebb and flow of congressional pressure for
unilateral troop withdrawal from Europe continues in

evidence. Congressional mood in the early 1980s was reminiscent of a decade earlier, except, perhaps, that there were signs of still greater determination and support for limiting U.S. troop strength in Europe than at the time Senator Mike Mansfield introduced his amendment.

In other respects, too, the situation described in 1977 underwent changes by the early 1980s. The budgetary picture turned bleak once again, and divisive trends in the Western alliance became more prominent.

9. Although some progress may have been made toward the reconciliation of discrepancies between Western and Eastern estimates of Warsaw Pact troop strength, the data problem in essence has remained intractable. Its resolution hinges on the exercise of political will by both sides.

In October 1979, Leonid Brezhnev announced that the Soviet Union would unilaterally withdraw 20,000 troops and 1,000 tanks from the German Democratic Republic within the span of twelve months. The stated intention of his maneuver was to deter the NATO powers from proceeding with long-range theater nuclear force (LRTNF) modernization, rather than to speed up MBFR negotiations. Although NATO rejected this type of quid pro quo, the Soviet Union proceeded with the planned removal of troops and announced its completion ahead of schedule. Clearly, an action of this sort cannot be properly considered by the West in the framework of MBFR. Moreover, the West has since claimed that as many and perhaps more troops than had been taken out have been reinfiltrated into units of the Soviet Forces in Germany.

10. Differences have been narrowed but not eliminated. Both sides have shown great ingenuity in seeming to modify their positions without actually doing so.

11. The Warsaw Pact has accepted the principle of a common ceiling for the residual forces of the two sides.

12. The Western principle of collectivity also appears to have been implicitly accepted by the Warsaw Pact.

13. For a time, the 50 percent formula appeared to be on the way toward acceptance. In the late 1970s, Chancellor Helmut Schmidt made several favorable references to it. The government of the Federal Republic of Germany, however, did not formally endorse the 50 percent formula, and NATO did not table it in Vienna.

The Soviet Union also showed interest in a 50 percent subceiling for any one country's troop strength within the alliance total. In the summer of 1983, the Warsaw Pact formally proposed the adoption of the 50 percent formula.

14. The idea of a European disarmament conference in the framework of CSCE has not faded. France has persistently championed it and the Soviet Union favors it. The conclusion of the second CSCE follow-up review conference in Madrid in early September 1983, after three years of negotiations, cleared the way for convening a Conference on Disarmament in Europe (CDE). President Reagan gave conditional approval to the holding of such a conference on March 31, 1983, and the NATO foreign ministers endorsed it in June 1983.

15. Chancellor Helmut Schmidt, address before the International Institute for Strategic Studies, London, October 28, 1977. German Information Center (New York, December 22, 1977); Survival, v. XX (January-February 1978): 2-10; and Wolfram Hanrieder, ed., Helmut Schmidt: Perspectives on Politics (Boulder: Westview Press, 1982), 23-37.

This speech by Chancellor Schmidt has acquired a certain notoriety. It has been widely interpreted, especially in the United States, as containing an urgent plea to counter the Soviet Union's menacingly growing Eurostrategic nuclear capability. Thus, Schmidt is credited as being the originator of the long-range theater nuclear force (LRTNF) modernization program formally embodied in the framework of the NATO "double track" decision taken in December 1979. The question whether this is the outcome Chancellor Schmidt had in mind remains unresolved.

3
Beneficiary of Detente

In the spring and summer of 1979, I was engaged in an extensive interview project in the Federal Republic of Germany, with the objective of ascertaining the security perceptions and concerns of a representative number of knowledgeable individuals. Between May and July, I conducted sixty in-depth interviews in seven cities: Berlin (eight), Bonn (twenty-four), Frankfurt (five), Hamburg (twelve), Köln (one), Mannheim (one), and München (nine).

The persons interviewed included nine elected representatives of political parties (five from the government coalition and four from the opposition); two parliamentary staff officials; six high-ranking civil servants; four military officers; eleven university professors; eleven researchers attached to scientific research institutes (some of whom also have university appointments, but do not qualify as university professors); fourteen media representatives (ten journalists and newspaper editors, and four radio and television journalists and editors); two retired diplomats; and one trade union official.

My sample included four women, and nine persons clearly identifiable as members of the "younger generation" (late twenties to late thirties), although I did not make it a point to ask anyone's age. Interviews were conducted orally, in German, English, or bilingually, in accordance with the preference of the interviewee. The average length of interviews varied between one-and-a-half to two hours. Two interviews were thirty minutes long, and one lasted three-and-a-half hours.

Identical broad questions were asked of each respondent about his (her) principal concerns for European security; assessment of the effects that the detente process has had on European security; priorities for topics that should be emphasized or de-emphasized in future East-West negotiations; and appraisal of the then emerging SALT II agreement (whether it would

contribute to or detract from European security).
Every respondent was also asked for an opinion concerning arms control initiatives (if any) that should be
taken to enhance European security; the relationship
between · arms control efforts and measures intended to
strengthen Western defenses; the manner in which the
Federal Republic could effectively promote European
security; the form in which a crisis might erupt in the
Federal Republic in the next five to ten years; and the
likelihood that such a crisis would occur.

The results were written up in a lengthy report,
which served as the basis of this interpretive essay.
Introductory comments in the essay on the status of the
West German economy and the impact that environmentalists organized as a political group (the Greens) could
have on future political stratification were derived
from information in other, public sources.

The Federal Republic of Germany on the Threshold of the 1980s
October 1979

On the threshold of a new decade, the Federal
Republic of Germany confronts the future with tempered
confidence. This does not connote a lack of realistic
concern for problems or, still worse, complacency, particularly about the country's security. It does be-
speak, however, the absence of pervasive anxiety that
the Federal Republic is in imminent danger of being
destabilized, either from the inside or from the outside.

The economy is robust: the rate of inflation,
even with steeply rising oil prices, is under 5 percent; unemployment, with fewer than 750,000 persons out
of work, is at a five-year low of 3.2 percent; and
exports are booming. The Gross National Product (GNP)
is registering a growth rate of 4.3 percent, as compared with 3.4 percent for 1978 (although a downturn to
2.5 percent or less is forecast for 1980). The Federal
Republic is vying with the United States as the ranking
exporting country in the world, and the Deutsche Mark
(DM) is second only to the dollar as a world trade
currency. The DM now accounts for some 14 percent of
international trade transactions, as compared with
52 percent for the dollar. Reserves of foreign currency, almost all in dollars, stand at a formidable
$48.7 billion, which is almost six times that of the
United States and twice that of Japan. Gold bullion
reserves in the Federal Republic account for another $4
billion, as compared with $22.3 billion for the United
States and $1.1 billion for Japan.

The social system is sound, industrial relations between labor and management are solid, and democracy is strongly entrenched. Formal political institutions and processes function effectively. They are not in danger of disintegrating in the face of adversity, as did those of the Weimar Republic under trying circumstances. The democratic spirit, of course, has to be further cultivated, and the people have not yet learned how to relax and enjoy life (as the French and Italians), nor how to handle adversary relations (as the English). But unless the social and economic fabric of society erodes badly—and that is not in sight—no significant polarization is likely to occur. Democratic rights will not be bartered for authoritarian leadership.

Terrorism has subsided, and the government can probably keep it from getting out of hand, should it rise again. Alienation from society on the part of a fairly large segment of adolescents could have disquieting, long-run implications, less because they are apt to flirt with radical movements and become politically engaged than because they are apathetic. In the foreign policy context, this means that they are disinterested in the United States and although indifferent toward the Soviet Union, susceptible to its propaganda claims.

Extremist parties—right and left—have fared badly in elections and are not a factor on the political scene. Neo-Nazism is a hollow specter; communism has minuscule appeal. The major parties are well established and cater to stable constituencies. The rise of environmentalists, organized as a political group and participating in electoral contests, however, is observed warily. Environmentalists do not bear a pronounced resemblance to traditional radicals (although they may draw some of their supporters from these circles), but, more importantly, they emotionally champion a cause which encompasses staunch opposition to the development of nuclear energy for peaceful purposes.

Even modest successes by environmentalists could profoundly affect the political landscape. The loss of just a few percentage points at the polls could drastically influence the standing of major parties. An October 1979 election to the parliament of Bremen, the smallest but not the least important of the eleven federal states, may be a harbinger of things to come. Here environmentalists obtained 5.14 percent of the vote and qualified, for the first time anywhere, for representation in the state legislature. In this instance, they cut into the electoral strength of the conservative Christian Democratic Union (CDU) and the liberal Free Democratic party (FDP) in roughly equal proportions. Each one of these parties lost two seats in the state legislature.

Environmentalist political groups (Greens) cut into the electoral strength of established parties, and have a significant effect on distribution of power.

Apart from affecting the delicate balance of national political power, environmentalists could have a major impact in the development of alternative energy resources. Considering that the most likely cause of an internal crisis would be a massive deterioration in the energy supply, the denial of nuclear power to the Federal Republic's industrial machine could have far-reaching consequences in the long run.

Severely impeded flows of energy and raw material supplies are feared as the gravest potential threats to the country's stability and security. Apart from developing domestic sources of energy to mitigate the effects of a protracted international energy crisis, the Federal Republic must also exert far greater efforts than in the past to expand and improve the quality of its relations with Third World countries (including OPEC). It needs to secure adequate energy and raw materials, as well as markets for exports. Despite high sounding words, remarkably little has been done along these lines. North-South problems have been neglected. They must urgently be addressed in the near future, and not just with a narrow view to economic considerations. For the energy situation could also trigger regional conflicts outside Europe, although it is by no means the only potential source of such conflicts. These could involve the superpowers and spill over into Europe. It is in the eminent interest of the Federal Republic to assume a greater responsibility for mitigating regional hostilities, particularly in the Middle East and Africa.

Direct military aggression against the Federal Republic is not an acute threat. In an otherwise volatile world with many potential flash points of war, Central Europe is an oasis of stability. A reasonable balance of forces exists, despite the Warsaw Pact's conventional military superiority and the Soviet Union's appreciable advantage in numbers of middle-range (Eurostrategic, long-range theater) nuclear weapons. The growing military power of the East is a matter of concern, but not the cause of immediate alarm. In the long term, these trends have disquieting implications and have to be attended to by a judicious mix of defense measures and arms control initiatives.

Disparities in the area of conventional military power have existed for a long time, and force relations have not deteriorated. The superior quality of NATO armaments helps to balance the quantitative advantage the Warsaw Pact has in troops and armaments (particularly tanks), although this qualitative edge is a gradually diminishing asset. Still, under existing and foreseeable conditions, the numerical superiority of the East is not a sufficient guarantee of quick and easy victory. Depending on the response of the West, the attackers would suffer substantial damage which they cannot a priori estimate with any degree of accuracy. A surprise attack, which might be tempting because it would hold out the best promise of success, simply could not be mounted. The numbers of troops and quantities of equipment involved would be too great to escape timely detection, giving the West adequate warning to mobilize.

Imbalances in the area of Eurostrategic nuclear capability are more pronounced, although they too are not entirely of recent origin. They are due both to the buildup of Soviet missile forces and the withdrawal by the United States of its land-based middle-range missiles from Europe in the early 1960s. What is new is a marked qualitative improvement in the Soviet Union's middle-range nuclear strike capacity. The new SS-20s, which are replacing the SS-4s and SS-5s, are mobile and have a MIRVed warhead. A gap has been created in NATO's deterrent between the strategic nuclear umbrella and the conventional military shield, reinforced as it is by tactical nuclear armaments. The existence of such a gap is, by definition, a source of weakness, although it is not clear exactly how the Soviet Union would exploit it. The gap should be closed as expeditiously as possible. Appropriate Western defense measures should be combined with East-West negotiations, aimed at creating an overall nuclear balance between East and West, rather than strict parity in the middle-range nuclear potential of the two sides in Europe. Not even hardliners believe that it is necessary or desirable to match the Soviet's Eurostrategic arsenal on a one-to-one basis.

As long as the West retains a flexible deterrent that is credible, military aggression on the part of the Soviet Union does not appear likely. Should the West become so weakened as to be unable to retaliate effectively, either because it is militarily incapable (which is almost unimaginable) or because it has lost its will (which is feared as a possibility), the direct use of the military as an instrument of aggression would not be necessary. The West would succumb to political pressure backed by force.

Various motivations and objectives are attributed to the Soviet leaders, and these run the gamut from ideologically determined designs on world dominion to practical considerations of the requirements of national defense, in the face of several hostile power configurations along the borders or in the vicinity of the USSR. Soviet leaders are not likened to Hitler or Genghis Khan. Rather, they are seen as rational (if within the context of their own rationality, which does not necessarily coincide with ours) and calculating persons who persistently seek advantages in a variety of ways, but preferably short of risking national suicide. The Soviet leaders are essentially low-risk

takers who would not precipitously launch war, especially since they still remember the close brush with
defeat and the destruction which their country experienced in the last war.

The military serves the Soviet Union primarily as
a potential or actual instrument of political pressure.
The impact which Eastern military superiority is meant
to have, and to a large extent does have, is political
and psychological and must be dealt with accordingly.
Quantities of arms alone are far from sufficient for
this task, although a certain amount of evidence of
adequate manpower and armaments at the disposal of the
West is indispensable. The emphasis, however, is on
the perceptual factor, on the political and psychological aspects of the problem. How skillfully the problem
is handled is up to the West.

The threat from the East can be managed. In the
course of some ten years of detente, the Soviet Union
has come into a more realistic focus. It has become
less mysterious and, by the same token, less menacing.
It is an unattractive model and suffers from many
structural shortcomings. It appears to have so many
internal problems and such difficulties in properly
controlling its East European allies that the expansion
of its influence--short of war--lacks plausibility.

Judging by the experience of the past few years,
the ability of the Soviet Union to exert decisive
political pressure on the Federal Republic is severely
limited. It has become clear that the Soviet Union
cannot dictate to others. Western democracy has proved
itself as a model both in resolve and in attractive-
ness. There has been an increase in confidence
throughout Europe and especially in the Federal Republic of Germany. A major source of this confidence is
the Federal Republic's intimate involvement in the
Western alliance. This is the strongest guarantee of
the Federal Republic's security, and participation in
the alliance is the determining factor in the Federal
Republic's foreign policy orientation. Everything
else (including relations with the German Democratic
Republic, which are sui generis and are of great importance to the Federal Republic) is subordinate to and
derives from alliance relationships. The Federal Republic is determined to contribute optimally to the
military strength and the social, economic, and political cohesiveness of the alliance, and it is at great
pains to give no cause to any of its members to distrust Germany's motivations, ambitions, and objectives.

As a general rule, the Federal Republic does not
wish to play an obvious leadership role in alliance
councils, because it realizes that lingering suspicions
of Germany survive in the memory of many people in
neighboring countries. These suspicions are part of a
historic legacy which the Federal Republic has not been

able to shed and which is likely to persist for some
time to come. The burdens of this legacy are gra-
ciously borne, and the constraints that it imposes on
the scope of foreign policy initiatives are scrupulously observed.

Precisely because the Federal Republic is so
deeply ensconced in the Western alliance and so heavily
dependent on it for its own security, evidence of
instability in the alliance is viewed warily. Social
upheavals and economic crises affecting one or another
West European country could pave the way for the Soviet
Union to promote discord in and among these countries
and capitalize on their malaise to gain greater influence over them. The Federal Republic can be helpful in
stabilizing faltering economies, but it is less able to
hasten West European economic integration and political
union. And it is helpless in exerting any influence on
American policy makers. It can only hope that they
will evolve their foreign policy and conceptualize
their global military strategy consistently with perceptions prevailing in Bonn.

In a sense, the Federal Republic is more preoccupied with the state of relations which it has with
the United States than its relationship with the Soviet
Union. The main reason is that the Federal Republic is
one-sidedly dependent on the efficacy of the American
nuclear deterrent. A close and harmonious relationship
with the United States is the sine qua non of the Federal Republic's existence.

Yet in recent years, the Federal Republic has been
often bewildered by the "incalculability" of American
foreign policy. The reliability of the American nuclear deterrent has become questionable, and the purposes of American policy in Europe are not as clear as
they once were. Will the United States honor its
commitments in the 1980s and 1990s as it has in the
past? Doubts that exist do not reflect an assessment
of America as militarily weak. Agitation and agony in
Washington over SALT II is little understood. From the
German vantage point, the military strength of the
United States is not inferior to that of the Soviet
Union, and SALT II does not bestow advantages on the
Soviet Union in the bilateral superpower context. It
does help to maintain parity between the strategic
arsenals of the superpowers and provides a considerable
certainty of expectations for both. The Protocol (to
SALT II), which temporarily limits cruise missile range
and deployment, and the noncircumvention provisions (of
SALT II), which could be differentially interpreted and
give rise to disputes, are troublesome but of minor
importance. It is the very concept underlying SALT II
that is most disturbing. The mutual paralysis of the
two central systems does have deleterious repercussions
on Europe.

[handwritten margin note: FRG more occupied with the U.S. specifically the nuclear umbrella]

[handwritten note at bottom: Doubts of U.S. commitment to its deterrent power and the appearances of ebbing military strength.]

The differentiation between central systems on the one hand and Eurostrategic systems (or theater nuclear forces) on the other hand, which is inferred in the Federal Republic as implicit in SALT II philosophy, connotes a decoupling of the defense of the continental United States from the defense of Europe. This represents a drastic--though not wholly unforeseen--change in what was believed to be American strategic doctrine and thinking, and it substantially reduces the effectiveness of the American nuclear umbrella protecting the security of Western Europe.

SALT II is objectionable in principle, but it is supported for two main reasons. First, it is seen as a necessary transition to SALT III, in the compass of which it is hoped that ways will be found to restore a viable, unified concept of integrated Atlantic defense. Second, failure to ratify SALT II would probably revive a cold war atmosphere between the superpowers. This would engender all manner of undesirable manifestations in Europe (not just in East-West relations but in internal politics) and in the relationship with America, which would be held responsible for the deterioration of the international climate.

The restoration of a viable, unified concept of integrated Atlantic defense has very high priority in the Federal Republic of Germany. It involves the so-called "grey area" of Eurostrategic nuclear weapons. But the problem is not addressed in identical terms in Washington and Bonn. In Washington, the issue is seen largely in military terms and quantities of weapons; in Bonn, the conceptual and political aspects of the problem outweigh strict military-technological considerations.

Conceptually, the issue of Eurostrategic nuclear arms must not be approached in isolation, for if it were, it would tend to lend additional credence to a fragmented Atlantic defense. European security would not be appreciably enhanced by the existence of a separate European-based nuclear capacity, which in any event would remain under American control. On the contrary, the dangers of decoupling the defense of Europe from that of the United States, which exist under SALT II, would be exacerbated. A war conceivably could be fought without endangering the American mainland. The destruction of the Federal Republic, however, would be a certainty, and this is not an acceptable option.

Politically, it is essential for NATO to demonstrate an ability to arrive at collective decisions rapidly and resolutely, through genuine processes of consultation among the members of the alliance. Time is of the essence, but NATO should not trap itself in a time bind of its own making. The setting of artificial, early deadlines for decisions is not the mark of decisiveness nor of superior statesmanship. It gives the Soviet Union gratuitous advantages. Irresolution or abrupt reversals in decisions that had been agreed on (or thought agreed on), however, should be overcome. NATO has had several bad experiences with faulty decision making. The Federal Republic in particular has been victimized by the ill-fated multilateral force (MLF) initiative in the 1960s and again by the neutron bomb fiasco in 1978. A third failure, regarding middle-range nuclear weapons, might be fatal to NATO. The alliance would lose credibility with the Soviet Union and with the populations of its own member states.

An effort to plug a hole in the Western defense system should not be allowed to become the source of discord in the alliance. A period of twelve to eighteen months would not be too long before coming to a well-prepared decision, particularly in view of the uncertainty surrounding SALT II ratification and forthcoming electoral campaigns in 1980 in the United States and the Federal Republic of Germany. Due attention should be paid to the sensitivities of all member states about quantities and types of weapons and their deployment. For example, it would be intolerable to station land-based missiles capable of reaching the Soviet Union in one country alone. What is the military rationale for introducing them? Are they to serve a counterforce or countervalue function? The Soviet Union is certain to target them, thereby increasing the vulnerability of the area where they are located. The Soviet SS-20 missiles, by contrast, against which these Western missiles are supposed to provide a deterrent, remain invulnerable because they are mobile and cannot be targeted.

The question also arises if the Federal Republic can actually accommodate new major armaments on its territory. Where will they be located? How much disruption of the natural environment will they entail? The West German landscape is even now fairly crawling with troops and armaments. The country is a veritable place d'armes. In an area that is approximately twice the size of New York State (or two-thirds that of California), there are over 700,000 ground troops. About half of these are Bundeswehr; the rest are contingents of NATO member states, including France.

Public opinion, domestic political concerns of elected officials, and budgetary limitations must be taken into account. The reaction of the Soviet Union, which also has legitimate security concerns, must be carefully gauged. If possible, the introduction of middle-range nuclear weapons by NATO should not have an escalatory impact on the arms race in Europe, but it should serve as an inducement for arms control and reduction. More and better arms of and by themselves do not necessarily buy greater security. Security

consensus should not be confined to the military
field.

Yet the evidence is that there are substantial
differences in prevailing security concepts on the two
sides of the Atlantic. The concerns of Europeans are
not well understood in Washington and are given short
shrift there. American policy is dominated by narrow
military considerations of security, and it does not
sufficiently value the political, economic, and psychological components of security which are increasingly
prized in the Federal Republic.

Similarly, American attitudes toward detente differ sharply from those of the Federal Republic. The
euphoria that characterized the early phases of detente
has given way to far more modest expectations. Although it has not produced millennial results, it did
open the door to a whole range of foreign policy options which have benefited the Federal Republic, particularly (but not exclusively) by facilitating the
regulation of the Berlin issue and the management of
the division of Germany.

There is no doubt that the Federal Republic has
been the chief beneficiary of detente and continues to
have a high stake in its preservation. A return to a
confrontational relationship with the Soviet Union is
unthinkable. But European detente, though different
from superpower detente and to some extent independent
from it, is considerably affected by the climate of
superpower relations. A deterioration in these relations (such as might ensue from the failure of the U.S.
Senate to ratify SALT II, or from other indications of
American hostility and distrust toward the Soviet
Union) would redound to the disadvantage of the Federal
Republic in many ways. Should the Soviet Union become
more truculent in its dealings with European states,
the Federal Republic would be particularly menaced:
pressures on West Berlin would certainly increase; the
relationship with the German Democratic Republic would
be undermined; human rights achievements, laboriously
attained and consisting for the most part of eased
conditions of travel and communication between the two
German states, might be nullified; and the scope of
contacts with other East European states might have to
be curtailed. But from the Federal Republic's point of
view, it would be almost as unpropitious if the Soviet
Union sought to redress a worsening superpower relationship through a major campaign directed at improving
relations with West European states. The Federal Republic would be once again the prime target of such
overtures which, under the conditions, would be difficult to fend off.

In sum, the Federal Republic does not want to bear
the brunt either of Soviet anger or of Soviet thrusts
for friendship. It does not cherish having to play the

part of the honest broker vis-a-vis the Soviet Union, mitigating the impact of U.S. hostility and distrust, or, conversely, promoting better relations with the West on behalf of the Soviet Union. Least of all does it want to be put in the position of a battering ram against the East.

For the Federal Republic, a stable and balanced relationship between the superpowers, in the spirit of competitive cooperation, tends to create optimal conditions in which the possibilities of improved East-West relations in Europe can be explored.

Washington and Bonn are at odds about other contemporary European issues as well, many of which can be subsumed under detente. They include specifics about human rights policies (although the differences in approach to these have been substantially narrowed) and the uses of CSCE as an instrument for the promotion of expanded and improved interaction among European states.

The Vienna talks on Mutual and Balanced Force Reductions (MBFR) are, perhaps, in a special category of their own. While there is an unusually high degree of cooperation and genuine mutual understanding between the delegates of the two countries on the working level, there are wide divergences of interest in and comprehension of the issues at the highest levels of the respective governments.

The personalities of office holders are at all times an important element in determining the climate of relations between countries. It would be wrong, however, to emphasize the influence of this element to the exclusion of longer-range trends. These reflect the cumulative impact of both subjective and objective factors bearing on the identification of interests by the leaders of the respective countries, and the mutual perceptions they have of each other.

There are, at present, obvious difficulties of communication between West German and American leaders. But the communications gap has been growing for some time, and its scope transcends the small community of officials in Washington and Bonn. The two countries have drifted apart. Some believe that in the Federal Republic this is largely a function of generational change. The attitudes of younger people (roughly between the ages of thirty and forty-five) toward America are distinct from those of their elders.

Older persons, whose memories and political activity hark back to the years immediately after World War II, had been totally awe-struck by the United States in their youth. They acquired a strong emotional attachment to America and unquestioningly accepted American leadership in world affairs. And well they might have. America was a shining example of democracy at its best and was a generous benefactor of

View of America:
Older folks remember U.S. post-war role.
Younger people have less contact, and less
warmth towards U.S.

their country. Younger people today, products of a
different era and different circumstances, tend to be
more dispassionate and objective--not to say criti-
cal--in assessing America's virtues and failings. They
have also had less exposure to American life, have
relatively few contacts with Americans, and have little
familiarity with the workings of American political
institutions. Many do not speak English. Moreover,
the America they observe from afar is much less attractive and less assured in its leadership role than the
America of thirty or even twenty years ago.

Generational differences, however, must be evaluated with discernment. For example, some younger people speak almost flawless English without having stud-
ied in the United States, and some older persons in
responsible positions have no command of English whatever. Older people, too, have experienced a certain
degree of disillusionment with the United States, and
the knowledge they exhibit of the American political
process reveals a less secure grasp on the realities of
politics in the United States than one would think.

Young and old share feelings of apprehension at
the prospect of still further estrangement between
their country and the United States. They grope for
ways of reestablishing an extensive and vibrant dialogue as a means of overcoming perceptual problems
they feel lie at the root of policy differences. They
are at a loss, however, how to devise improved channels
of communication. They do not harbor feelings of hostility toward the United States, and they show no trace
of evidence of a disposition to change the terms of the
relationship with America. Since they recognize that
their country does not have a viable alternative, they
usually acquiesce in American policies that affect the
Federal Republic.

It is arrant nonsense to impute to the Federal
Republic any proclivity for striking a deal with the
Soviet Union (a new Rapallo), for engaging in an arcane
exercise of "self-Finlandization," or even for aspiring
to achieve a reunification of the two German states.

Reunification is simply not regarded as a practical possibility in the foreseeable future, even if it
were desirable. In the view of most West Germans, it
is highly questionable if reunification holds any tangible benefits for them. It could be achieved only at
the price of neutrality, and a neutral Germany would be
a defenseless, emasculated entity. A gradual rapprochement between the two German states, however, is a
distant objective being pursued at all deliberate
speed. The road to it is seen leading through a substantial easing of tensions in Europe, which would
eventually allow for a greater improvement in relations
between the two German states.

Reunification seen as not practical and
presently undesirable. Gradual rapprochment
is however important.

The danger of Finlandization--or, still worse, self-Finlandization--would become real only if the United States substantially withdrew its protection from the Federal Republic. Under such circumstances, the threat of a new Rapallo might also arise. The Federal Republic is not likely to flee into the clutches of the Soviet Union; it can only be driven into the arms of the Russian bear.

This does not mean that the Federal Republic is not intent upon prudently exploring ways to improve relations with the Soviet Union and the East European Communist regimes. It believes that there is much to gain and little to lose from a course which aims to achieve a mutually acceptable modus vivendi. It is a mistake on the part of the United States if it confuses a policy of judicious restraint, that seeks accommodation on reciprocal terms, with appeasement.

In dealing with the Soviet Union, arms control negotiations have highest priority for the Federal German government; for after ten years of detente, there is a sobering realization that little progress has been registered in this crucial area of endeavor. The Federal Republic's engagement with the Soviet Union in this arena has been especially perfunctory. In the view of the German government, the confidence-building potential of the arms control process should be better utilized to help build a security partnership between East and West. Arms control should not be regarded as an end in itself but as a means to an end, and the process should be institutionalized as much as possible.

MBFR, which focuses on the relationship between the conventional military forces of NATO and the Warsaw Pact, bears more significantly on the security interests of the Federal Republic than any other ongoing arms control discussion. The successful pursuit of these negotiations remains an objective of utmost importance. These talks in Vienna, which have dragged on through six dreary years without yielding visible results, have actually achieved a great deal. Conceptual differences between the two sides have been substantially narrowed, and they have agreed on some mutually acceptable principles--such as parity--after reductions have taken place. The seemingly intractable data issue, which pertains to the actual number of Warsaw Pact troops currently in the reduction area, may be closer to resolution. Other contentious issues, involving the phasing of reductions and the definition of collectivity, are also in advanced stages of reconciliation. Even to date these talks have served an excellent confidence-building function, not in the least because they have brought together the political *and* military representatives of the two alliances.

Economic relations with the East are not likely to expand spectacularly. Early optimism about a major breakthrough was disappointed, and expectations of future possibilities have been commensurately scaled down. The human rights area is not one which the Federal German government is inclined to probe extensively for possible exploitation, because it is considerate of the sensitivities of the Eastern regimes. These regimes have great difficulty in coping with human rights issues. They will perforce react defensively to any Western overture which they perceive as a threat to their stability. The destabilization of the Eastern regimes--which in turn would engender a backlash against efforts to improve relations with them--would be counterproductive. For the Federal Republic, the human rights issue centers in the relationship with the German Democratic Republic. There it is being promoted in a variety of ways, patiently and with infinite forbearance.

Although it would be farfetched to say that there is a unanimity of views in the Federal Republic about major foreign policy problems and prospects, the consensus about them is far broader than would appear from reading or viewing West German media or listening to public statements by some politicians.

The media in the Federal Republic, much as in America, tend to exaggerate, polarize, and sensationalize issues. Politicians seek publicity and willingly lend themselves to "exploitation" by the media. This is true particularly of members of the opposition parties (CDU/CSU) who have been out of power for over a decade, and who need issues over which to attack the government coalition (SPD/FDP). To make their point, spokesmen for these parties are not above exacerbating problems beyond their true dimensions. The state of "inner-German" affairs (that is, the relationship between the two German states) is particularly susceptible to emotional airing in public forums. Other favorite topics for scaremongering are, of course, the Soviet military threat (with special emphasis on the SS-20 mobile nuclear missile) and the danger to the Federal Republic's security that lurks in the light-hearted--if not irresponsible--negotiating tactics on the part of the government in the Vienna MBFR talks.

The temptation to magnify policy differences between challenger and incumbent in an election year is likely to be almost irresistible, especially in view of the personality of the challenger, Franz Josef Strauss. A crafty and aggressive tactician, he skillfully but ruthlessly bullied the parties supporting him to nominate him as chancellor candidate. (He threatened to split the CDU/CSU coalition unless he were nominated.) He is also an irascible person, often incapable of controlling his anger in public.

This is not to suggest that the parties in the government coalition and those in opposition do not hold different views on many issues. These include the sequence between procurement and deployment of middle-range nuclear weapons and negotiations with the Soviet Union on limiting these types of weapons; the potential usefulness of economic leverage to induce the Soviet Union either to desist from pursuing certain objectives or to cooperate more responsibly; and the intensity with which the human rights issue should be pressed.

It is most improbable, however, that any party charged with responsibility for making and implementing policy would depart measurably from the present course. For one thing, domestic political expediency dictates that all parties steer clear of extreme positions, which would not be acceptable to significant portions of the population. For another, severe external con-straints curtail the choice of policy options. Fi-nally, articulated opposition to what the government is now doing is a function of political rivalry and dis-trust of the judgment and motivation of some Social Democratic leaders (such as Herbert Wehner, Egon Bahr and even Willy Brandt), rather than a reflection of fundamental policy differences. Basically, the conser-vatives chafe at having been kept out of power for a decade and want to get back in.

By and large, there is widespread confidence in the Federal Republic that from the secure vantage of membership in the Western alliance the country can manage to cope with any threat emanating from the East. There is little illusion, however, that substantial improvement in relations with the East can be brought about easily and rapidly. On the contrary, there is every expectation that the status quo will not be susceptible to major change. Glacial progress is prob-ably the best that can be hoped for.

Soviet power may not be directly projected into Western Europe, but it will make itself felt. It will certainly not recede from Eastern Europe. Dealing with the Soviet Union will become more complicated and dif-ficult. The Kremlin leaders will use the formidable power at their disposal to threaten and cajole (and use proxies, such as the East Germans), in an unrelenting effort to loosen the bonds between the Federal Republic and the United States and to drive a wedge between the Federal Republic and its West European allies.

The turn of the decade from the 1970s to the 1980s is not a propitious time for histrionics nor one for glorious and heroic exploits. Rather, it is a time for a policy of small steps that place a high premium on the application of superior managerial skills to coax the gradual evolution of a European order. Cohesive-ness of the Western democracies must be furthered, and conditions must be fostered which allow basically in-compatible systems to live together in greater harmony.

4
Resurgent Confrontation between East and West

The opinions expressed in the interviews which I conducted in the Federal Republic of Germany in the summer of 1979 probably reflected a more optimistic appraisal of current and foreseeable conditions in Europe than the cold facts warranted. A North Atlantic Assembly report issued late in 1979 contained a more sober assessment of the results and prospects of detente, but it strongly recommended that the policies associated with detente be continued.[1] The fall of 1979 and the winter of 1980 witnessed a rapid deterioration of East-West relations, particularly between the superpowers.

By early fall, it was clear that SALT II (signed ceremoniously in Vienna on June 18 and sealed with a presidential kiss) was in deep trouble in the United States. Ratification by the U.S. Senate was increasingly in doubt, provided that President Jimmy Carter had the courage to submit the accord for public scrutiny in the first place. The attack on and occupation of the American Embassy in Tehran in November compounded the burdens under which the American administration was laboring. The approach of 1980--a presidential election year--weighed heavily on the occupants of the White House. They desperately needed to show strength and determination in the conduct of foreign policy in order to dispel impressions of their indecisiveness, unpredictability, and ineffectiveness.

An upcoming NATO decision on long-range theater nuclear force (LRTNF) modernization was just the right opportunity. The stage was set by Leonid I. Brezhnev's bold bid (in the context of a major policy statement he made in East Berlin on October 6) to deter NATO from implementing its LRTNF modernization plans. Fearing that under these circumstances even a temporary postponement of the NATO decision would be widely interpreted as capitulation under Soviet pressure, the White House was determined to push ahead on schedule. On December 12, NATO adopted a "double track" decision on

LRTNF, which called for deployment of new U.S. systems
in Europe in the event that negotiations with the Soviet Union failed to yield satisfactory results by the
end of 1983. The first item in this chapter (written
in October 1979) addresses problems connected with the
timing of the NATO decision and counsels a course of
action different from that which was subsequently
taken.

The Soviet Union's invasion of Afghanistan on
December 21, 1979, precipitated a full-blown crisis of
the international system. President Carter hastened to
invoke sanctions against the Soviet Union, and Soviet-
American relations plummeted to a new low. West-West
relations were also affected, and the partners on the
two sides of the Atlantic showed the strains of the
differences between them. The Europeans, fearful of
the consequences of a renewed superpower confrontation
that would render their existence more precarious,
arrived at different interpretations and reached different policy conclusions from the United States. The
hubbub over Afghanistan had not yet subsided when a
major upheaval in Poland began to unfold, threatening
the stability of the Communist system in that country
and thus the fragile balance of East-West relations in
Europe.

It was in such circumstances that a new, tough,
conservative, and ideologically strongly anti-communist
administration came to power in the United States. The
second entry in this chapter (which was originally
delivered as an address before the World Affairs Council of Northern California in San Francisco, one day
after the presidential election in 1980) contains an
analysis both of the effects the crises in Afghanistan
and Poland have had on relations between the United
States and Western Europe, and of the qualities of
American leadership that would be conducive to
strengthening the cohesiveness of the Western alliance.

The third essay deals with the international repercussions of the events in Poland in December 1980,
some four months after the beginning of the Polish renewal. In the fourth essay (written in January 1981),
I briefly delineate what foreign policy challenges
President Reagan confronts upon taking office, and how
these could be met most effectively.

The fifth essay (written in early fall 1981) was
delivered originally as an address before a gathering
of young European conservatives in Köln. In it, I
attempt to assess the military and political consequences of the NATO "double track" decision. By then
this decision had become the focal point of confrontation between the superpowers. It had also triggered
widespread anti-nuclear agitation throughout Western
Europe and adversely affected the development of transatlantic alliance relations.

The final essay in this chapter evaluates the international repercussions of the events in Poland for a second time, in February 1982, about two months after the declaration of martial law there. In both instances, my observations about the Polish events were made in addresses delivered before the Commonwealth Club of California in San Francisco.

United States Response to the Threat of the Soviet SS-20
October 1979

The news from Washington clearly indicates that both the administration and the Senate seriously misinterpret the attitude of the European members of NATO toward long-range theater nuclear force (LRTNF) modernization and SALT II. As a consequence, the North Atlantic alliance is well on its way to being driven into yet another crisis, which may be the most serious in its thirty years. The Carter administration seems to act on the premise that the European countries expect it to show strength and leadership ability by ramrodding through a hasty program of LRTNF modernization, calling for the deployment of 572 American middle-range nuclear missiles on the continent. The Senate, in turn, appears irked that the European countries seek to exert pressure on it to ratify SALT II, by threatening not to endorse LRTNF modernization unless the controversial agreement limiting strategic arms is adopted.

Perhaps it is a reflection on the hysteria that has gripped Washington that our European allies are so thoroughly misunderstood there. In Washington, issues are seen almost exclusively in military terms and quantities of weapons. In European capitals, the conceptual, political, and psychological aspects of problems outweigh narrow military-technological issues.

In Europe, despite some disagreement about the sequence in which NATO defenses should be strengthened and pertinent arms control negotiations with the Soviet Union should commence, there is a strong consensus that rearmament and arms control efforts must be intimately linked. Even the hardest of hardliners do not envisage matching the Soviet arsenal of middle-range nuclear missiles one-for-one. The figures most often mentioned are approximately 200 missiles, a number which is deemed sufficient to deter the Soviet Union and adequate to constitute a negotiating base with the Russians. A gap has opened up in NATO's defenses by virtue of the superiority which the Soviet Union has attained in middle-range nuclear missiles, particularly through the deployment of the SS-20 mobile and MIRVed missile. The Western objective is to plug this gap, but to do so with the aim of reducing tensions in Europe rather than escalating the arms race.

As Europeans see it, there are many outstanding problems to be resolved and several options to be explored. While time may be pressing--the Soviet Union installs SS-20s at a rapid pace--NATO should not put itself under self-imposed deadlines. No harm would come from postponing a decision on LRTNF modernization until after the elections in the Federal Republic of Germany (September 1980) and in the United States (November 1980), and until after the removal of uncertainties about the status of SALT II in the U.S. Senate.

In the view of Europeans, the rush to buy more arms and to spend huge sums for them--even if they are better than the old ones--should not be an end in itself. The procurement of arms should be contingent on the uses for which they are intended. Security concerns should not focus singlemindedly on military issues; political considerations should also be taken into account. The Soviet military threat must, of course, be judiciously assessed. But legitimate Soviet security interests should not be disregarded, and interaction with the Soviet Union should not be restricted to the military field. Among European NATO members, the primacy of politics is axiomatic. Politically, it is essential for NATO to demonstrate a quiet confidence in its capacity for defense and in its ability to arrive at reasoned collective decisions through genuine processes of consultation. Discord would have adverse effects on the alliance; still worse would be additional evidence of irresolution expressed in sudden reversals of decisions that had been taken. The memory of the "neutron bomb" fiasco is firmly imbedded in the consciousness of Europeans. In their opinion, anything resembling this experience could have fatal consequences for NATO, which would lose all credibility with its own constituencies. Since the chances are quite high that a decision about the deployment of U.S. middle-range nuclear missiles in Europe reached now might have to be modified or even rescinded in the future, it would be best not to act in haste.

There is an integral connection between the ratification of SALT II and LRTNF modernization. To proceed with plans for LRTNF modernization prior to a clarification of the fate of SALT II in the U.S. Senate would not be logical. Actually, Europeans have grave reservations about SALT II, but not for the same reasons as the opponents of the treaty in the Senate. Europeans do not share the fears of those Americans who believe that SALT II bestows a military advantage on the Soviet Union. What does perturb the Europeans, however, is their sense that the philosophy underlying SALT II implies a decoupling of European (theater) defense from the defense of the continental United States and thus diminishes the security of Western Europe. Their interest in the approval of SALT II is conditioned by fear that failure to ratify the treaty would reintroduce a cold war atmosphere into the superpower relationship, which would be detrimental to European detente, and by hope that ratification of the treaty would set the stage for SALT III negotiations. In the compass of SALT III, the conceptual flaws contained in SALT II could be remedied, "grey area" (theater nuclear) problems could be broached and an integrated Atlantic defense concept restored.

By contrast, the deployment of large numbers of American missiles, over which the United States would retain full control, would give an escalatory impetus to the arms race. Some question the rationale underlying the introduction of the missiles. Aimed at military targets, they are bound to be ineffectual, since the SS-20s are mobile and are by definition not targetable. Aimed at civilian targets in the Soviet Union, the new missiles would invite retaliatory targeting of densely populated urban areas in Western Europe.

In the estimation of Europeans, the Soviet Union could not be induced to negotiate about the reduction of middle-range nuclear missiles in the absence of a SALT II agreement.[2] Responsibility for this adverse development would rest squarely on the shoulders of the United States.[3]

The insistent campaign now waged by the Soviet Union against the deployment of middle-range nuclear weapons in Europe just about assures the adoption of the American plan at the NATO ministerial meeting in mid-December. To act otherwise would appear to be yielding to Soviet pressure. Yet the logic of the argument favoring a postponement of a decision about deployment has intrinsic merit, and it would be regrettable if several governments felt forced to approve an action despite their better judgment, simply to avoid the impression that they have succumbed to Soviet threats.

The administration is obviously in no position to change its course, even if it wanted to. Another change in course would be interpreted at home and abroad as further evidence of weakness on its part, and it would probably doom such chances as SALT II still may have, to gain approval in the Senate. Only the Senate itself can come to the rescue, for it need not be afraid of being accused of catering to the Soviet Union.

The Senate would perform a superior act of statesmanship if it rose above partisanship and urgently called on the administration to desist from pressing forward with LRTNF modernization, at least until after the debate on SALT II has run its course on Capitol Hill and a vote on the treaty is in hand. And in subsequently ratifying SALT II (which it should, on the merits of the agreement as written), the Senate might well consider passing a sense resolution. In it, the Senate should affirm this country's commitment to the concept of a unitary, integrated Atlantic defense. It should direct the administration to implement appropriate measures to close such gaps as might have arisen in the defense structure of the North Atlantic alliance, acting prudently and in concert with its European allies in this endeavor.

Effects of the Crises in Afghanistan and Poland on Relations between the United States and Western Europe
November 1980

As late as the summer of 1979, few Europeans expected that the stability of relations on their continent would be so rudely jolted and so soon by developments outside the European region. Most of those with whom I had talked, however, had indicated that if stability in Europe were to be undermined in the foreseeable future it would most likely result from some upheaval outside Europe, in one or another area of tension around the world, but probably the Middle East. Although the Iranian revolution was in full progress by then, few anticipated the shattering showdown that was to ensue between the regime of the Ayatollah Khomeini and the administration of President Carter by November 1979, and no one in my memory cited Afghanistan as a flash point that would threaten to set aflame the entire international system.

The Soviet invasion of Afghanistan represented a watershed in East-West relations. At the same time, it precipitated a profound crisis in the Western alliance. Troubling problems that had been developing for some time, but went largely unattended, suddenly became acute policy questions that required prompt answers. The most trenchant question posed by the Soviet invasion of Afghanistan was whether detente was divisible. Could detente be preserved in one regional setting while it was being demolished in another? Or put differently, could the Western alliance honor detente relations in Europe, while the Soviet Union blatantly violated them on a global scale?

Thoughtful analysts had anticipated that the 1980s would be a difficult decade in East-West relations.

But few, if any, foresaw just how difficult the new decade would turn out to be and how soon heightened
difficulties would arise. The invasion of Afghanistan
underscored the reality of growing Soviet military
capabilities and reflected--in Western eyes--a commensurate confidence of the Soviet leadership in these
capabilities. American observers had viewed with increasing dismay the ever-expanding scope of Soviet
military involvement in far away places--such as Angola
and Ethiopia--through proxies, advisors, and impressive
logistical support. But the invasion of Afghanistan
was the first time that Soviet troops had been used
openly in an area which, although adjacent to the Soviet Union, was considered in the West as lying outside
the sphere of direct Soviet dominance. Thus, the invasion of Afghanistan was the capstone confirming a trend
that had long been apparent. It was seen as particularly ominous because it seemed to signal the drive of
Soviet power southward, toward the Gulf region, which
is an area of crucial importance to the West and about
which the West is understandably sensitive.

For these reasons and perhaps others, the Soviet
initiative in Afghanistan seemed to call for a strong,
coordinated alliance response and a reassessment of the
relationship with the Soviet Union. The United States
reacted unilaterally and in great haste. President
Carter condemned the Soviet Union and invoked sanctions
against it. He called on the European allies of the
United States to join in condemning the Soviet Union as
an international outlaw and in punishing it through
sanctions and boycotts. Many Europeans expressed grave
concern about the military and political consequences
that the projection of Soviet armed forces into Afghanistan would entail. But they tended to be critical of President Carter's precipitous reaction as hys-
terical and incongruous on the part of a weak and
indecisive leader. He had proved incapable of resolute
action against revolutionaries in Iran who had occupied
the American Embassy and held a large number of Americans hostage.

The reactions of West European powers were not
identical. France, at least in the person of President
Giscard d'Estaing, appeared most anxious to maintain a
dialogue with the Soviet Union. The French president
journeyed to Warsaw in the spring of 1980 for a meeting
with Soviet President Leonid I. Brezhnev. The Federal
Republic of Germany was overtly supportive of the
United States. It joined in boycotting the Moscow
Olympics, but the West Germans were not enthusiastic
about the prospect of drastically revising their Ostpolitik. Most Europeans advocated a firm but measured
reaction that was tempered by a desire to preserve stability on the continent and not to sacrifice in a fit
of anger those gains that had been made under detente.

1st direct and open use of Soviet military, and in a region believed to be outside of Soviet's sphere of influence.

Different reactions between the U.S. and Europe underscore difficulties in the alliance.

Divergent approaches by Americans and Europeans to a common problem reflected different experiences they had with detente, different vantages from which they viewed East-West relations and also, mutual irritations between their leaders.

Personality clashes between the American leadership and European political leaders (particularly West Germans) were a contributing factor to the acerbity that marked transatlantic relations in the second half of the seventies. Important as these subjective factors were, they alone did not account for the pronounced policy differences between the United States and its West European allies that became evident under the impact of the Afghanistan crisis. But crises often have a way of bringing into sharp focus disagreements and clashes of interest that remain more or less submerged in conditions of normalcy. The relationship between the United States and Western Europe had been changing throughout the 1970s. In my opinion, the transatlantic partners were gradually drifting apart. This was, perhaps, an inevitable but at least not surrising consequence of detente.

Briefly put, in Europe detente took roots and appeared to be bearing fruit. Processes of political and economic interaction between East and West multiplied and became more intimate, and some headway was made, even in the murky area of human rights. Europeans from both sides frequently engaged in exchanges of opinion in a variety of forums. The dialogue between them acquired substance and led to the identification of common interests which they mutually nurtured. By contrast, in the United States the early bloom of detente wilted and gave way to skepticism about the value of detente. (A one-way street is how presidential candidate Reagan characterized it in 1976, and in the same year the term itself was dropped by President Ford from the official vocabulary of the U.S. government.) Simultaneously, a suspiciousness spread throughout America about the motives and goals of the Soviet Union--a suspiciousness which to me seems of unparalleled depth since before World War II.

Signs of steadily growing Soviet military might, while American military capability stagnated and even declined, led to preoccupation in the United States toward the end of the decade (well before Afghanistan) with this adverse trend. It became obvious that imbalances in the military relationship between the United States and the Soviet Union had to be redressed. Similar considerations applied to force relations between NATO and the Warsaw Pact. At President Carter's initiative in 1978, NATO adopted a Long-Term Defense Program (LTDP) which called for a sustained real growth of 3 percent in defense spending. Soviet intervention in Afghanistan accentuated the urgency to shore up

[handwritten margin note, left side, vertical:] Europe had much more real political, economic and human rights gains through detente while the U.S. became more disenchanted

[handwritten note, bottom:] The military imbalance between U.S. and USSR prompts Carter to ask for increased defense spending by NATO allies in 1978.

Western defenses globally and regionally. Afghanistan
also introduced a new dimension into alliance security
in the form of "out of area" contingencies. In the
past year, the United States has demanded that its
European allies do more in terms of both assuming a
greater share of the defense burden in Europe and
providing direct assistance to the United States in the
Gulf area.

European members of NATO have reacted to these
American initiatives with reservations. For one thing,
they have felt that their military expenditures did not
diminish in the 1970s, and it is therefore unfair to
request they help make up for the slack in U.S. military expenditures in this period. For another thing,
they have been extremely leery about extending the
military responsibilities of NATO beyond the original
geographic confines of the alliance. Some have given a
strict constructionist interpretation to the defensive
nature of the alliance, and they have been at pains to
avoid any semblance of planning for or eventually participating in "out of area" military operations.

In the heated political atmosphere engendered by
Soviet military intervention in Afghanistan, the Western alliance did not succeed in forging appropriate
coordinated policies with which to counter the new
Soviet challenge. The Soviet Union was spared meaningful retaliation. On the contrary, it was able to
exploit policy differences among the NATO allies to its
own ends until late in the summer of 1980, when internal developments in Poland introduced a new, unforeseen
factor into the European situation.

The Polish drama, the full dimensions of which are
still unfolding, is the result of a unique combination
of circumstances that brought the Polish Communist
system to the brink of disaster and the Polish people
to a state of hopelessness and despair. The economic
and moral bankruptcy of the system was so evident in
mid-July when I visited in Poland that I was left won-
dering how the Soviet Union could have allowed things
to deteriorate to such an extent. Indeed, I questioned
if the Soviet Union had been aware of conditions in
Poland as they really were. If it had, why did it not
assist the Polish regime in heading off a crisis? If
it had not, what sort of interest did it have in Poland
and how tightly and effectively did it exercise control
over developments there? These are serious questions
worthy of more than passing attention, for they shed
some light on the capabilities and the policy processes
of the Soviet Union. Two bankruptcies, or near bankruptcies, of fraternal countries--Afghanistan, a new-
comer, and Poland, a charter member of the community--
within the span of one year would appear to be too
much. There is a message in these events, a message
that the Kremlin cannot afford to ignore by labeling

Poland's link w/ Afghanistan:
- two Soviet backed regimes hit the skids
in the same year
82
- Soviets couldn't afford military involvement
in both at the same time.

the events as evidence of nefarious machinations by imperialist powers to undermine the socialist international system.

The Polish events were not a direct outgrowth of
the Afghanistan crisis; but there may be a connection
between them, insofar as the Soviet Union is reluctant
to become militarily involved in two countries at the
same time. Under these circumstances, the Polish
workers may have more latitude than they would otherwise have to press the Communist party to fulfill their
demands.

A definite Soviet response to the Polish developments has not yet emerged. The Soviet Union is undoubtedly conducting a policy review and is weighing
its options. On the one hand, it cannot let developments get out of hand. On the other, it must weigh the
risks of military intervention most carefully. Precedents in Hungary (in 1956) and in Czechoslovakia (in
1968) have little relevance for the current situation
in Poland. Apart from other factors, in 1956 and 1968
the Soviet leadership was not constrained by considerations for the preservation of a structure of peace,
however tenuous that structure may be. Now the Soviet
Union does have a substantial investment in European
detente. Readiness to risk forfeiture of this investment would serve to expose both the fears that torment
Soviet leaders and the persistent inability they have
to countenance peaceful change in the rigid model of
socialism which they developed and imposed on Eastern
Europe. It would also reveal their sinister determination to cling to the miserable gains they made by force
of arms at all cost.

Judging by what I could glean from conversations
in Moscow and Leningrad a little over two months ago,
when there was not much public knowledge of the upheavals in Poland, the Soviet leadership is in a grim
mood. Far from being optimistic about the successes of
its foreign policy, it feels itself once again under
heavy external pressures. These pressures compound the
very serious economic difficulties which exist and
which should be attended to. President Brezhnev's
recent public statements bear testimony to a clear
awareness at the highest level that the Soviet economy
is running down, but these statements do not contain
clear-sighted remedies that could cure the ills from
which the Soviet economy suffers.

The Polish events even more than Afghanistan introduce a note of uncertainty into the processes of
East-West interaction in Europe. A number of adverse
developments since the outbreak of unrest in Poland
have already taken place. So far, the foremost victim
has been West German Chancellor Helmut Schmidt, whose
cautious but deliberate Ostpolitik has suffered serious
reverses. A carefully planned program of summit

meetings with East European Communist leaders had had to be scrapped.

It is clear that Soviet military intervention in Poland would abruptly terminate detente in Europe. Shielding Western Europe from possible Soviet aggression would be at a premium. (I myself believe that the Soviet Union will desist from precipitating such a crisis in Europe, as long as it possibly can.) But even short of such a drastic development as a Soviet invasion of Poland, the United States under a new president has a great opportunity to display qualities of leadership that would inspire confidence among its allies and regain respect for America among its friends as well as its foes.

In the 1970s, Europeans became very skeptical about America's leadership qualities. The crisis of leadership in the Western alliance significantly affected the drift in American-European relations to which I had reference. The problem that arose could not be attributed solely to the personal attributes of American leaders, nor to the differential character of East-West relations in Europe and between the United States and the Soviet Union. The relationship between America and Western Europe has changed. While Western Europe has remained dependent on the United States for military security, it has emancipated itself from American tutelage, politically and economically. Furthermore, Europeans are no longer in awe of the United States. If anything, they tend to be too critical of our faults, although they know us much less well than they think. In my opinion, failure to take the changed West-West relationship into account is responsible for many difficulties with which the alliance has to contend. I am not sure if the United States is equal to the task of developing the needed qualities and style of leadership. But I do know that the president-elect has a mandate to instill a genuine unity of purpose in the Western alliance.

Ingredients of enlightened American leadership in the North Atlantic alliance include: recognition that reciprocity must govern relations among members of a democratic alliance; adherence to the practice of vigorous and forthright consultations in the alliance; tolerance for the specific problems of individual alliance members and forbearance in accommodating diverse interests within the common purpose of the alliance; reaffirmation of a defense doctrine that dispels apprehensions about a disaggregated regional defense strategy in which Europe might be sacrificed; and unequivocal commitment to a strategy of deterrence.

Looking ahead, the United States must convince its allies that it is steadfast and reliable in protecting them from military aggression and simultaneously supportive of their prudent search for constructive

interaction with the East, even in the face of deplor-
able Soviet actions. An abiding challenge in Europe is
to find infinitely fine balances between resistance to
Soviet threats on the one hand and appeasement of the
Soviet Union on the other hand.

Should the new administration not be able to capitalize on the mandate it has, the rift between America
and Western Europe would widen to the detriment of
both. The United States is a global power with commensurate responsibilities. Europeans must understand
this and accommodate themselves accordingly. But
America's destiny remains inextricably iterwoven with
that of Europe. If we allow the fabric of this common
destiny to be torn asunder, we would indeed court a
decline of what is loosely--but not inaccurately--
called Western civilization.

Eastern Europe—Still Unresolved
December 1980

A specter is haunting Moscow--the specter of trade
unionism in Poland. It is clear even now that the
Communist world will never again be quite the same.
How different it will be remains to be seen.

This year, which began in the chill winter shadow
of the Soviet invasion of Afghanistan, may yet end in
the frost of Soviet military intervention in Poland,
although I myself strongly doubt that. I do not believe that the Soviet Union will take such a fateful
step.

To intervene for the third time (not counting the
East Berlin riots in 1953) in the affairs of a fraternal East European Communist country brought to the
brink of collapse would entail far-reaching adverse
consequences, affecting the Soviet Union's status in
the world and shaking it internally as well. Not that
the Soviet Union might not be tempted to intervene--but
the tangible costs of intervention are predictably
greater than either in 1956 or in 1968. Both the local
situation and the international configuration are
vastly different.

Before I continue with an assessment of the international implications of current developments in Poland, I should like to note briefly that another potential crisis period in an area related to the Soviet
Union (but not technically considered an East European
country) passed without any evidence of destabilization
in the first part of the year. I have in mind the
death of President Tito of Yugoslavia. To date, there
has been no discernible pressure on the part of the

Soviet Union to gain more influence in Yugoslavia or to
direct that country from its path of development,
which, after all, is a variant of socialism not consistent with the Soviet model. Internally, the transition
from Tito to his successors was smooth, thanks in part
to the lingering death of the president, which allowed
new men to run the affairs of state while he was still
present. The transition was gradual. The people were
not confronted with an abrupt change and had no reason
to panic. By clinging to life for an inordinately long
time, Tito helped to create conditions of optimum stability for the transition.

The main sources of difficulties are economic.
The country is in the throes of a protracted economic
crisis (which may yet give rise to political strife)
between more- and less-developed constituent republics
of the Yugoslav Federation. This could have a divisive
influence on the fragile federal constitutional and institutional structure, without a charismatic leader to
hold it together. Internal strife might provide opportunities for interference in the country's affairs by
outside parties.

Massive economic problems (problems that may in
fact be intractable) are also at the base of the events
that have rocked the Polish Communist system to its
foundations. The fuse that set off the unrest was the
announcement last summer of differential rises in the
price of meat. Of and by itself, this was not an un-
reasonable action by the government. The price of meat
and other staples had been kept artificially low by direct government subsidies running into billions of
zlotys a year; and in the country's straitened economic
circumstances, the authorities felt they had to cut
back on such expenditures. The strikes that ensued in
various industrial centers, however, reflected not just
irritation over the question of meat supply and meat
prices. They vented the pent-up frustration of the
workers--and indeed the whole population--over the
general crisis of the Polish economy and, more than
that, the corruption and ineptitude of the Polish Communist leadership which had managed to plunge the country into a state of moral torpor, hopelessness, and
despair.

Events could not have developed as they did had it
not been for precedents of high promises and dashed
hopes in 1956 and 1970, which were accompanied by major
changes in leadership, and an additional serious confrontation between workers and the government over food
prices in 1976. The decade of the seventies, in particular, was one in which the flaws of the system
became increasingly apparent. Taking advantage of a
relatively large degree of freedom to discuss and
criticize, various groups during this period proceeded
openly to analyze the problems besetting their country.

Roots of Polish crisis: - general crisis of economy and poor
leadership
- lost hopes of 1956 and 1970 for change
- open discussion of problems

The level of consciousness of the entire population
rose to unprecedented heights. By 1980, it was no
secret from anyone that the economy was in desperate
straits, due to faulty planning, mismanagement, low
productivity, and rather bad luck as a consequence of
changes in the world economy, which Poles could not
have anticipated.

Economic indices for 1979 showed the Polish
economy in regression. The Gross National Product
(GNP) actually diminished by a small fraction. Few
people, however, had any ready solutions to offer for a
way out of the crisis, and the prevailing national mood
in the country in the summer of 1980 was one of utter
disorientation. Things could not go on in the old way,
but no one knew how to change them and who should
replace the old leadership.

It is against this background that the dramatic
events of the past few months have to be judged, especially if one looks ahead and contemplates how things
will sort themselves out. Our focus tends to be on
power alignments and power relationships, and these are
of tremendous importance. The real test of the viability of changes, however, will be whether or not they
will succeed in rescuing Poland from economic collapse.
To this end, all forces within Poland will have to
cooperate responsibly, the authorities as well as the
workers. Poland faces a long period of economic reha-
bilitation in which demands on the system will have to
be scaled down and efforts redoubled, in order to sustain the economy through improved planning, management,
and labor productivity. The international community
will, of course, also play a significant if not decisive role in shaping the country's future.

The repercussions of the Polish events have already been amply evident throughout Eastern and Western
Europe. In Eastern Europe, Communist leaders have been
at pains to draw attention to substantial differences
between the conditions prevailing in Poland and in
their respective countries.

Nevertheless, the Polish crisis gives renewed
evidence of a general systemic failure which applies to
all Communist regimes. But it also has its unique
features, just as the Hungarian and Czechoslovak crises
had in their time. It would be a mistake on our part
to think otherwise and to draw invidious conclusions.
The perceived threat to the other East European regimes
varies. Their responses to date have also varied in
accordance with a number of circumstances: their perceptions of the threat which the Polish events represent to them, the degree of direct influence exercised
over them by the USSR, and the intensity of hostility
or residue of sympathy toward Poland felt by their
leaders and their peoples. Not surprisingly, in criti-
cizing Polish developments, Czechoslovakia and the

German Democratic Republic have been most hostile; Hungary, somewhat restrained; and Romania, quite perfunctory. Most interesting, however, is the sudden discovery by all Communist regimes, including the Soviet Union, that trade unions play an important role in socialist systems. Assessments of the performance of the trade unions in representing the interests of the workers have not been uniformly laudatory. Among the Warsaw Pact countries, there is evident concern over the hitherto untried and untested potential of these exclusive organizations of the workers.

In Western Europe, international repercussions of the Polish events have been felt particularly by the West Germans, whose Ostpolitik has already suffered some setbacks as a result. Summit meetings between Chancellor Helmut Schmidt and Edward Gierek of Poland as well as one with Erich Honecker of East Germany were called off. West-East German relations, which seemed to thrive on the aftershock of Afghanistan, have gone into reverse gear in the aftermath of the Polish events. The East German regime has been particularly anxious to insulate itself from potentially harmful influences stemming from both its neighbors: Poland and the Federal Republic of Germany.

The Polish drama is still unfolding, and the full extent of its domestic and foreign policy impact remains to be revealed. It poses enormous problems, far more serious ones than the Hungarian and Czechoslovak crises ever did.

The Soviet Union is confronted with a dilemma of immense proportions. The cost/risk calculus attendant upon any policy option is uncommonly complex.

Military intervention must be tempting. It would "solve" certain problems by forcefully stopping a drift away from the accepted model of socialism. But at what price? Can the Soviet Union be militarily engaged in Poland and Afghanistan simultaneously? How much bloodshed in Poland would have to be anticipated and how much can the Soviet Union safely absorb? How would Poland develop under Soviet bayonets? Would Soviet military intervention be able to prevent the collapse of the economy? What economic burdens would the Soviet Union have to bear to help restore the economy, and what effects would a collapse of the Polish economy have on the Soviet Union and the rest of Eastern Europe? Would the setbacks not be well nigh fatal? What would the Soviet Union sacrifice in tangible and potential gains in its relations with Western Europe? It is not image alone that is involved, but the reality of a laboriously built structure of political, economic, and other types of interaction among European states from which the Soviet Union has benefited, and from which it expects to derive continuing benefits. European detente (including the prospect of arms control) is

squarely on the block here. Can the Soviet Union jet-
tison a policy which it has so assiduously cultivated
for over a decade? How would its status vis-a-vis the
rest of the world be affected? Would its opportunities
in Third World countries improve or decline? And would
its confrontation with China grow more or less intense?

The Soviet Union must also carefully consider the
consequences of nonintervention. Will the Polish contagion spread? How will it affect the cohesiveness of
Eastern Europe? What effect will it have on the Warsaw
Pact's military capabilities? Will it endanger Soviet
security interests?

The Kremlin leadership faces some very hard decisions and may find itself in a no-win situation. So
far, despite obvious and blatant intimidation, it has
taken no actual untoward steps and has in fact shown
remarkable restraint. It has tried to head off a
showdown and give Poland enough scope to solve its
problems or hang itself, as the case may be. Instead
of using military force, the Soviet Union will focus on
containing internal developments in Poland so that they
do not undermine the country's socialist foundations.
It will also concentrate on limiting the damage that
the spread of the Polish contagion could inflict on
other Communist systems in Eastern Europe.

The West is also faced with difficult choices. It
must seek to head off Soviet military intervention,
since it cannot realistically envision meeting it head-
on by means of arms. Simultaneously, it must make it
unmistakably clear to the Soviet Union how high the
price of intervention would be, in terms of East-West
relations. But the West must also decide how to proceed in regard to Poland if there is no Soviet military
intervention, for the burden of salvaging the Polish
economy will rest preponderantly on Western shoulders.
Poland's enormous hard currency debt is a cardinal
factor in the country's ability to survive. What does
prudence dictate: more massive aid, and under what
conditions and to what ends? Or less aid on very
stringent terms?

The West must refrain from providing the Soviet
Union with a credible pretext for intervention and thus
cannot encourage those forces whom it would normally
favor. Yet the West cannot abandon championing human
rights and political freedom, and it cannot help to
stabilize a Communist regime at the expense of the
welfare and well-being of the subject population of
such a regime. To translate the conceptual desiderata
and caveats into practical and viable policy terms will
not be an easy task, but the challenge is matched by
opportunities. America and its allies could demonstrate their unity of purpose and their determination
to safeguard the integrity of the Western alliance by

closing ranks around a common program. At the same
time, they could contribute to the stabilization of
conditions in Europe by devising creative initiatives
designed to preserve the modest though real gains
scored in East-West relations in the preceding years.
The interests of all have to be taken into account; the legitimate security concerns of all must be
duly observed. The dramatic upheavals in Poland are a
monument to the indomitability of the human spirit.
Recently won gains must not be allowed to be trampled
on. Adversity and prosperity almost always coexist in
a dialectical linkage. It is incumbent upon all to
make every effort, through as much cooperation between
East and West as possible, to create the best opportunities for Polish developments to move in constructive,
rather than destructive, channels.

Reagan's Foreign Policy Options
January 1981

Although President Reagan confronts a multitude of
foreign policy challenges, he also has substantial
opportunities to turn a new, more promising page in our
world relations. In four years Jimmy Carter had for-
feited his chances, and there was no reason to expect
that he would have done better, had he continued in
office. That alone made Reagan's election worthwhile.
At worst, the new president will be feared or perhaps
despised abroad, and even that would be preferable to
being distrusted and laughed at as Carter was.
Machiavelli tells us if a choice has to be made, it is
better to be feared than ridiculed. At best, however,
Reagan could regain respect for and confidence in the
United States.
The president's instinct to be tough with the
Soviet Union is correct, as is his determination to
beef up our military capabilities. Such attitudes are
ultimately likely to make the Soviet Union amenable to
engage in serious, meaningful talks with us to achieve
a modus vivendi. Basically, the Soviet leadership is
awed by our enormous capacity to gear up for military
production, and it is fully aware of the disadvantages
it would have in an unbridled competition of arms with
the United States. The Soviet Union is beset by formidable economic problems at home and considerable political and military adversity on its borders. Diver-
sion of still greater resources to the military might
strain the economy beyond endurance. Of course, the
Soviet Union will exert itself to the utmost to keep

pace if it has no viable alternative, but given one, it
will seize it.

The opportunity, then, is to link the acquisition
of more military clout--which is an indispensable ne-
cessity--with a prudent and balanced approach to the
curtailment of Soviet expansionism and a mutually acceptable control of arms. The military clout we seek
should be appropriate to the contingencies with which
it would have to deal, or which it would be intended to
deter from occurring. More budgetary resources may
have to be allocated for these purposes, but precaution
should be taken that we do not succumb to a false sense
of greater security by simply expending greater sums of
money for more armaments. The money should be spent
wisely, with an emphasis on diversity and quality,
rather than quantity, of armaments. And in acting
tough with the Soviet Union in its global ventures,
care must be exercised not to confound decisiveness
with a penchant to humiliate.

The Soviet Union's obsessive preoccupation to
extract formal (treaty) recognition from us that parity
exists between the two superpowers has to be reconciled
with our own increasingly obsessive concern for the
retention or restoration, as the case may be, of our
national power. Equitable arrangements will come within reach if and when the respective sensitivities and
exaggerated fears of the two sides can be calmed,
without doing violence to sound precepts of adequate
defense capability to safeguard the national security
by both of them.

But the foreign policy agenda is not limited to
and should not be dominated by military considerations.
Political, economic, and communications components,
substantially neglected in the past, have to be up-
graded. The president can seize the opportunity to
broaden the gauge on which our foreign policy is conducted. An enumeration of all specifics would be tedious and in the given constraints of space, impossible.

China, the Middle East, energy, food--all clamor
for attention. Relations with Third World countries
generally have to be addressed head-on. We should make
certain that no one harbors illusions that we can be
kicked around with impunity. We should leave no doubt
about our opposition to restructuring the international
economic order by a drastic redistribution of wealth.
At the same time, we should signal to the developing
countries that we are prepared to expand and improve
relations with them, with due regard to their special
economic needs and consideration for their political
sovereignty, on the basis of strict reciprocity, mutual
benefit, and observance of each other's dignity.

The most promising opportunities for improvement,
however, exist in our relations with Europe and our
global communication effort.

Geographically, Europe remains the focal point of United States foreign policy. Our commitments there have to be ironclad, for our own fate would be more profoundly affected by changes in the European status quo than by any other development in the world. Yet the North Atlantic alliance has eroded over time, and the impact of Afghanistan at the beginning of 1980 accelerated the pace of erosion. The Soviet invasion of Afghanistan revealed just how far Europe and the United States have drifted apart in the period of detente, and it accentuated divisions among the NATO partners. The fault does not lie exclusively on either side of the Atlantic, but the fact that America is grossly misunderstood by its closest allies and friends --and that the United States in turn substantially misconstrues their motives, interests, methods, and objectives--is cause for alarm. President Reagan can begin remedying this situation by demonstrating stead-fastness of purpose and by exercising a new style of leadership.

There is reason to believe that our European al-lies are now more receptive to American initiatives than they were, earlier in 1980. The Polish events have had a sobering effect on Europe. The Soviet Union has not intervened militarily as yet and most probably will refrain from doing so, but the tensions created by the Polish events have not subsided. Indeed, they are likely to mount. The future of Poland itself hangs in the balance and is not likely to be resolved soon. Meanwhile, the reverberations of the Polish events can be felt throughout Eastern Europe and have a chilling effect on trends for closer cooperation between East European and West European states, particularly the two German states. Although the structure of detente has not yet been shaken to its foundations, it has once again been forcefully brought to people's attention just how fragile detente is. The moment is propitious for a reappraisal of options, so that the gains made during the past decade in interaction among European states from East and West are not wantonly sacrificed. At the same time, efforts to safeguard and promote these gains should not undermine a firm determination to resist aggression and to avoid appeasing a would-be aggressor by humoring him. America can reassert its leadership in Europe by acting in concert with its allies rather than in isola-tion from them; by consulting with them instead of issuing commands; and by adapting itself to a diversity of specific interests among them, which do not contra-dict the general purposes of the North Atlantic alli-ance. The alliance need not march down a narrow path in lockstep. Problems may be handled on different levels and in various ways, preferably by prior agree-ment within the alliance. If that were the case, the cohesiveness of the alliance would be strengthened, and

this might well be the most important objective for
which America should strive. The effectiveness of alliance policies vis-a-vis the Soviet Union might also
be enhanced, and that, too, is a desirable goal to be
pursued.

Our global communication effort is perhaps the
weakest link in our foreign policy, in an era of information revolution in which the volume of communication
is growing by leaps and bounds and processes of communication among nations are gaining unprecedented importance. America's inability to project a proper image
to the world and its propensity not to listen to what
others are saying seriously impede the development of
an effective foreign policy.

The president has an opportunity to arouse public
awareness of international affairs (which is an indispensable precondition for more meaningful communication
with the outside world) and to raise the professional
quality of communication by revitalizing the ailing
United States International Communications Agency. The
president's own predisposition to engage the Soviet
Union in spirited ideological struggle demands an urgent upgrading of what traditionally has been a sagging
national effort. But the task surpasses by far the
mere necessity of conducting an ideological crusade
against the Soviet Union.

We must make ourselves more understandable to the
world and learn to understand the world better. Otherwise, we run the risk of being increasingly isolated,
while our friends and foes carry on an ever more inten-
sive dialogue among themselves and identify a growing
number of interests they have in common, to the detriment of the United States.

Effective communication is the cutting edge of a
successful foreign policy. To recall Napoleon's dic-
tum, there are only two types of power in the world:
the power of the sword and the power of ideas, and of
the two, the power of ideas is the stronger.

Military and Political Implications
of NATO's "Double Track" Decision
on Modernizing Long-Range Theater Nuclear Forces
October 1981

The so-called long-range theater nuclear force
(LRTNF) modernization decision (I prefer the German
term Doppelbeschluss, which is at once succinct and
inclusive), adopted at a special meeting of the foreign
and defense ministers of the member states of the North
Atlantic Treaty Organization on December 12, 1979, is a

milestone in the organization's search for credible military deterrence, coupled with an earnest striving for accommodation between adversary alliances through arms control negotiations. It is perhaps the most fateful decision NATO has taken and was prompted by perceived adverse changes in the East-West military balance in Europe.[4]

The provisions of the Doppelbeschluss, on the one hand, call for the acquisition of 572 land-based long-range (but not intercontinental) missiles, including 108 Pershing II's and 464 ground-launch cruise missiles (GLCMs) and their deployment in five European countries (the United Kingdom, Italy, Belgium, the Netherlands, and the Federal Republic of Germany). On the other hand, they call for initiation of arms control negotiations between the United States and the Soviet Union for the attainment of an equitable Eurostrategic balance.

The perceived changes in the military balance between East and West in Europe which gave rise to the LRTNF decision reflected a persistent drive for armament modernization in the Soviet Union under the aegis of detente. One of the products of this drive was the SS-20 missile. Because of its characteristics--mobility, MIRVing (three independently targetable warheads with a charge of 150 kilotons each), distance, and accuracy--the SS-20 represented a qualitative increment, if not a quantum jump, in the Soviet's long-range (Eurostrategic) missile capability. NATO did not possess an adequate counterpart. Seen against the background of a corollary change in the relations between the central systems of the superpowers, the advantages which the Soviet Union could derive from the SS-20 appeared particularly menacing. For the existing parity between the central systems of the United States and the Soviet Union neutralized the classical U.S. deterrent and eroded the very foundations of Western Europe's security, which had been predicated on the assumption that a clear-cut nuclear superiority existed on the part of the United States.

Some people argued that the qualitative improvements in Soviet missile capability due to the SS-20 were overstated and that fears of a paralysis of the central system of the United States under the given conditions were exaggerated. The SS-20 was little more than an updated version of the SS-4 and SS-5, which had been targeted on Europe for two decades. The alleged selective, thus counterforce, capacity of the SS-20 with warheads of 150 kilotons each was perhaps more fictional than real, considering the densely populated industrial environment of Western Europe.[5]

Nevertheless, it seemed prudent to try to close the gap in the Western defense structure which had thus arisen between battlefield weapons--whether they be

*[handwritten top margin: The problem as J. sees it:
1.) Divergence between NATO's battleground capability and US strategic capability
2.) Gap not consistent w/ NATO strategy of flexible response
3.) Decoupling of Europe from U.S.]*

[handwritten left margin: Europe hoped successful negotiations might release NATO from deployment. US however planned to deploy regardless.]

conventional or nuclear--and American strategic systems.   Discontinuity in the defense capability of NATO
was not consistent with the NATO strategy of flexible
response, which requires a finely articulated, gradually escalated reaction to Warsaw Pact aggression.   It
also threatened to decouple the defense of the United
States from those of Western Europe.   The specter   of
decoupling haunted European leaders, for they dreaded
the prospect that a future European conflict would be
regionalized.

The measures propounded by the NATO ministers
seemed inevitable.   Some have argued that the timing of
the decision was not felicitous.   Others have propounded precisely the opposite view.   To postpone the
decision until spring 1980 would have been politically
inexpedient, because of the impending electoral campaigns in the United States and the Federal Republic of
Germany.

Although the ministers did not act in haste, the
wording of the communique announcing their decision
left unclear the exact connection, in operational
terms, between the "two parallel and complementary
approaches" (parallel laufenden und komplementaren
Vorgehensweisen) which they recommended.   This lack of
precision made the decision susceptible to misrepresen-
tation as well as exploitation by hostile propaganda.
Nor were contingencies foreseen in the event that the
two approaches could not be satisfactorily linked.
Naturally, the ministers could not have anticipated the
chain of events that began to evolve less than a month
after their meeting in Brussels.   Still, they might
have been more circumspect.

The   fact that the unspoken premises on which the
allies acted when they adopted the LRTNF decision were
not identical has left in its wake a hidden, unfinished
agenda.   Europeans on the whole hoped that negotiations
would obviate the necessity of deployment by the end of
1983 when the new systems were slated to be ready,
while Americans were rather determined that a number of
missiles--if perhaps not all 572--would be deployed in
any case.   The communique itself strongly suggests that
one underlying assumption of its signatories was the
successful conclusion of a SALT II accord, that is, its
ratification by both superpowers.   Regulation of the
central systems would be followed by a similar process
in regard to theater systems, in the context of an ever
more inclusive structure of arms control measures.

Who can tell if NATO would at present be in a more
favorable situation if it had desisted from concluding
the Doppelbeschluss in 1979 or if the content of its
decision had been made more precise? That things would
be different is a fair assumption.

The consequences of the Doppelbeschluss to date
only faintly correspond to the expectations of its

architects. NATO has not been militarily strengthened.
If anything, the opposite is true. Its military position vis-a-vis the Soviet Union has deteriorated. The
Soviet Union's response to the LRTNF decision was to
speed up the rate of expansion of its arsenal of SS-20
missiles (though uncontrovertible proof for this contention is lacking).   Their number is said to have
increased from some 60 in 1979 to 200 or more in 1981.
Meanwhile, NATO's own middle-range missile capacity has
remained static--that is, zero. This is certainly not
the outcome the NATO ministers strove for.   Politically, in turn, prevailing circumstances have caused
the LRTNF decision to become the object of agitation
and strife that has rent the political structures of
several member states of the alliance and fostered
disunity within the alliance.   These are not results
one would deliberately plan.

In assessing the military implications of the
LRTNF decision, it is common practice to have recourse
to a numerical data base depicting the power relationship between NATO and the Warsaw Pact. It is futile to
search for precision in the numerical authentication of
one or another claim.   An exercise in arithmetic in an
article published in the West German weekly Die Zeit
illustrates the point.[6] According to this article,
NATO disposes of 548 launchers as against 690, 870, or
1,050, as the case may be, for the Warsaw Pact. Variations in the Warsaw Pact total are due to discrepancies
in counting the number of SS-20s, since the launchers
are allegedly reloadable and are outfitted with an
average of two or three missiles. My problem, however,
is less with the Warsaw Pact's inventory than with
NATO's.

Can all 548 launchers be properly included in the
NATO total?   Some 82 that are listed are under French
control.   They include 18 ground-launch medium- or
intermediate-range ballistic missiles (MRBM/IRBM) and
64 submarine-launch ballistic missiles (SLBM) but, for
unexplained reasons, 40 Mirage IV aircraft are omitted.
The missiles under French control are not subordinated
to the NATO command. Can it be assumed that they would
be automatically used in conjunction with a NATO nuclear response?   At the minimum, there would exist a
formidable problem of command and control coordination.
Another 114 launchers in the list represent an independent British national nuclear capability (50 Vulcan
bombers and 64 Polaris SLBMs).   To be sure, these 114
missiles are available to and closely integrated with
the NATO command structure. But can they be put in the
balance in the context of U.S.-Soviet LRTNF negotiations?

In contrast with the 548 launchers listed in Die
Zeit, in the spring of 1980 the defense minister of
the Federal Republic of Germany identified 386 NATO

French nuclear force not to be counted in NATO's # . and British force is only ostensibly so .

launchers, including (in brackets) 122 under French command: 64 SLBMs, 18 land-based MRBM/IRBMs, and 40 Mirage IV medium-range bombers.[7] Without the French contribution, the Ministry lists 264 NATO launchers, inclusive of the 114 British.

What accounts for the difference? Apart from insignificant variations which may in fact reflect changes in the inventory between 1980 and 1981, there are entire categories of systems listed in Die Zeit which are missing from the ministry's roster: 120 Starfighter F-104 aircraft, 30 carrier-based A-6E and A-7E bombers, and, perhaps most importantly, 40 U.S. Poseidon C-3 SLBMs.

The problem with some of these systems (F-104, A-6E, A-7E) is their short range, which really disqualifies them from the middle-range category. The problem with the Poseidon C-3 SLBMs is of a different order of magnitude. Basically, they are assigned (dedicated) by the United States to the NATO command and come under its jurisdiction, but they are also part of the American strategic arsenal and their utilization is foreseen in the eventuality of general war. They are covered by the provisions of the SALT I agreement. Should they or should they not be accounted for in NATO's panoply of middle-range missiles?

In sum, the picture is confusing. One might as well say that NATO's capacity consists of 150 U.S. F-111s as to quote any other figure up to 548. As for the Warsaw Pact inventory, the ministry flatly claims 1,320 launchers, well in excess of the highest figure in Die Zeit. Clearly, something is amiss.[8]

Who can vouch for the reliability of the data? How many SS-20s have been deployed: 150, 200, 250, or more? How many of them are targeted or targetable on Western Europe: two-thirds of the total (which is the most frequently cited figure) or more (depending on the exact location of sites east and west of the Urals)? Do SS-20s uniformly carry three warheads (as is commonly assumed in the West) or do at least some carry fewer than three warheads (as a Soviet spokesman recently implied)? Is the yield of these warheads invariably 150 kilotons (again, as is generally assumed in the West) or are at least some yields different, and perhaps higher (as the the above-mentioned Soviet spokesman also hinted)?[9]

This is not to say that the popular pastime of "bean counting" has no utility whatever. Rough numerical estimates, cautiously interpreted, do provide a basis for informed judgment. For example, the fact that in the contentious realm of land-based middle-range missiles the Soviet Union has an advantage of some 600 to 650 against 18 (all of the latter being French) or zero (if the French components are discounted) is not something one can dismiss as being

irrelevant.   The   imbalance may not be fatal,   but   in
principle it would appear large enough to warrant   rec-
tifying it.
     Under any circumstances, the judgmental element is
likely   to   be more important than raw   numbers.   More
than quantitative data have to be relied on in   estimating the East-West military balance.   Qualitative factors, such as performance characteristics (range, accuracy,   yield,   and   others),   weapons mix,   command and
control problems,   psychological and political   aspects
(perceptions, consensus, and will), and even accidental
elements   (malfunctioning   of   equipment,   unforeseen
changes in weather,   and human failure) have to be duly
considered.
     By what objective criteria does one determine   the
military   efficacy   of weapons systems?   What are   the
criteria of essential equivalence?   Must every   system
on   one   side be matched by an identical system on   the
other side?   Must there be a common ceiling for middle-
range missile systems as for troops under   MBFR?   What
differentiates   a   deterrent   capability   from   a   war-
fighting one?
     On   what basis does one assert that the   installa-
tion   of a system provides .greater security by deterring would-be aggression   or, on the contrary,   creates
greater   insecurity   by increasing   the   likelihood   of
preemptive first strike on the part of the adversary?
     How   valid   are contentions about the   dangers   of
decoupling America's defenses   from those   of   Europe
under one or another set of military conditions (a   gap
in   the   defense triad of escalating responses   in   the
context   of   a flexible response strategy or no gap   in
this   triad)?   Can   the danger of decoupling   be   adequately   defined   in strict military   linkages   between
battlefield,   Eurostrategic (middle-range), and central
(intercontinental) systems?
     This short list of questions is neither exhaustive
nor   inclusive.   I doubt that there are   any   absolute
certainties   concerning   the military   implications   of
LRTNF modernization.   The more so,   as nuclear weapons
are   regarded by most observers as being primarily   political   weapons,   particularly suited for intimidation
and not for the conduct of military   hostilities.   Yet
debate   about   the military implications of LRTNF   modernization is difficult to still.   It is conducted at a
high pitch of emotionalism with extravagant claims   and
counter-claims, charges and counter-charges.
     On balance,   one might venture a guess that   LRTNF
programmed   for deployment does have a deterrent potential,   by   raising   the threshold of   uncertainty   with
which Soviet strategists have to contend.   Should   the
Soviet   Union   contemplate war,   it would   probably   be
forced   to launch simultaneous,   coordinated preemptive
strikes   against   military targets in Europe   and   the

According to Zimmer, Euromissiles would be a deterrent to Soviet chiefs. They would have to launch at both US and Europe, and suffer the consequences or they could launch against only Europe, be retaliated by NATO missiles, and left in less of a position to face possible attack from the US, or China.

Therefore, it is doubtful that Europe would be in any more danger off a 1st strike.

NATO's deployment wouldn't be of 1st strike value. Can't get SS-20s or to not deploy sufficient number to justify Soviet retaliatory force.

United States. The complexity of such an endeavor would not augur well for success. A conflict limited to Europe, however, would elicit a response from NATO's LRTNF which would inflict substantial damage on the Soviet Union. The country would not necessarily be incapacitated or even crippled, but it would be at a comparative disadvantage vis-a-vis the United States (as well as other adversaries, such as China) that would have been left intact. Thus, from the Soviet point of view, the damage sustained would be unacceptable. Hence, wisdom would dictate prudence. The Soviet Union would be dissuaded from precipitating nuclear hostilities in Europe.

If the foregoing argument has any merit, it also serves to contradict the contention that LRTNF would expose Europe to the danger of a Soviet preemptive or first strike aimed at annihilating these installations, widely dispersed over a large area (although the Pershing IIs are slated only for the Federal Republic of Germany).

The argument that LRTNF is prima facie a first-strike weapon and thus threatens the military balance in Europe appears to have limited merit. For one thing, LRTNF does not have the range to destroy SS-20s stationed in the secure sanctuary of the Soviet Union, even if these mobile launchers could be reliably targeted. For another thing, the number of LRTNF would not suffice for a preemptive attack. The irreducible requirement for such an attack is at least a mathematical chance of annihilating the opponent's entire retaliatory capacity at once.

Soviet claims that LRTNF represents a new threat to the USSR cannot be taken at face value. LRTNF threatens the Soviet Union only as an improved means of retaliation, that is, as a more effective deterrent. Thus, LRTNF denies the Soviet Union an advantage it has carefully tried to nurture and which it has enjoyed for some time. This is analogous to diminished security and is probably so interpreted by the Soviet leaders.

Command and control problems pertaining to LRTNF are complex and vexing and give rise to justified concern. Yet in the main, the chances that land-based LRTNF could be engaged in an appropriate, timely, and effective manner, in the compass of a series of graduated responses to attack, seem superior to those of sea-based LRTNF. The latter would probably entail a longer reaction time, and coordination with other battlefield activity--from which they would be far removed--would be awkward.

The usefulness of LRTNF as a "bargaining chip" in arms control negotiations aimed at the reduction of Soviet middle-range nuclear capability is probably limited. Critics contend that the concept of developing systems as "bargaining chips" does not have a convincing record in such negotations.

98

[handwritten: Unlikely that the Soviets would back away from current advantage because of NATO deployment, not to mention prestige factor.]

Paradoxical as it may seem, the premise that NATO has to develop an LRTNF capability (arming) in order to be able to secure mutually acceptable control for this weapon system (disarming) is logically flawless. But is it efficacious? It is questionable if the Soviet Union would allow itself to be coerced to negotiate away a current battlefield advantage. If nothing else, prestige and pride would prevent the Soviet Union from negotiating "under the gun."

The NATO approach to negotiations is deficient in other respects as well, most importantly in having failed to develop a comprehensive negotiating concept. What should be negotiated? SS-20s, Pershing IIs, and GLCMs only, or other Soviet carriers as well, such as the Backfire bomber? What about the forward-based systems of the United States, which the Soviet Union has insisted must be integrally drawn into middle-range missile negotations? Should delivery vehicles (missiles and other carriers) or warheads be counted? How can warheads be verified? Should limitations be placed on the mobility of systems? What levels of deployment are acceptable? Should there be equal numbers on both sides or is a certain ratio satisfactory if the levels are sufficiently low, possibly to the point of having no middle-range weapons on our side in exchange for a drastic reduction of the existing Soviet arsenal?[10]

Since negotiations have not yet begun, we do not know how damaging the absence of a comprehensive negotiating framework might in fact be.[11] Delay in starting the negotiations, however, has been largely ascribed to the reluctance of the United States since late 1979 to sit down with the Soviet Union, and this is having widespread adverse political repercussions in the - Western alliance. These repercussions cannot be properly viewed as a direct outgrowth of the LRTNF decision, for they are the result of subsequent developments. Nevertheless, it is difficult to separate growing indignation in Western Europe over the delay in LRTNF negotiations from the general syndrome of uneasiness engendered by LRTNF modernization.

The political implications of the LRTNF decision are much more serious than the military ones. Obviously, this is not solely due to the fact that nuclear weapons are, in the minds of many people, political weapons primarily suited for intimidation. No amount of military capability would be of the slightest use to NATO if the Western countries could not properly engage this capability. Conversely, a strong political will would enable them to resist Soviet nuclear blackmail even with an inferior military arsenal.

The political fallout, if one may say so, attendant upon the LRTNF decision has been quite extraordinary. It seriously threatens to undermine the Western alliance by putting in question the very principle and purpose of NATO's LRTNF decision, as if Western

[handwritten right margin: Not so much a matter as military capability, but political will to deter a Soviet attack]

Subsequent political agitation explained by:
1.) Deployment here raised consciousness of
Europe and added to anxieties
2.) Negotiations on arms control have been
delayed

apprehensions based on fear of the unrestrained expansion of Soviet theater forces had not been then and
were not now justified, and as if the Doppelbeschluss
rather than Soviet aggressive behavior were chiefly
responsible for the deterioration of East-West relations.

Political agitation can be attributed to two major
factors. First, the LRTNF decision has raised to a
high level of consciousness in Western Europe the destructive potential of nuclear weapons and has caused
an upsurge of anxiety. Second, the implementation of
the arms control portion of the LRTNF decision has been
inordinately delayed by a chain of events that ensued
from the Soviet invasion of Afghanistan, which also
helped to seal the fate of an already moribund SALT II
agreement.

Differential perceptions among NATO allies about
the underlying motivation of the brutal Soviet invasion
of Afghanistan and concerning the application of sanctions against the offending superpower (which violated
the rules of the game as interpreted in the West)
exacerbated those tensions within the North Atlantic
alliance which had already been in evidence, and they
created new ones. Divisive trends between alliance
partners on the two sides of the Atlantic, which had
become apparent in the course of detente (especially
under the Carter administration), became more pronounced under the impact of crisis. The election of a
new, militant administration in Washington, determined
to make amends for past sins of omission in arms development and past sins of commission in the pursuit of
evanescent arms control objectives, further deepened
the fissures in the alliance. If Europeans restrained
their impatience with Jimmy Carter during an arduous
election year and showed at least grudging understanding for his reluctance to honor the portions of the
Doppelbeschluss calling for negotiations,[12] they did
not conceal their dismay at the palpable belligerence
of the new administration, its penchant for a massive
rearmament program, and its lack of enthusiasm for arms
control.

The tumultuous events since the adoption of the
LRTNF decision have been skillfully exploited by the
Soviet Union, not just by building up its own strength
while professing a readiness to negotiate, but by casting doubt on the good faith of the United States. In
the framework of a tightly orchestrated, widespread
propaganda campaign, the Soviet Union has played both
upon the suspicions of West European populations toward
the United States--which the tough talk and intransi-
geance of the Reagan administration seemed to confirm--
and the irrational but very real fears that prevail in
Europe about the prospect of any kind of war, let alone
a nuclear one.

Fanning the breeze as the Soviet Union has cannot
cause a fire, but it can help to build an existing
flame into a conflagration. That is what may be happening at present. This is not to lay all responsibility for the problems of the alliance at the door-
step of the Soviet Union, although much of the responsibility does rest there. Soviet behavior has un-
leashed the current international crisis and Soviet
propaganda seeks to reap its benefits.

Significant as the effort of the Soviet Union and
its Communist tools has been to foster anti-nuclear
agitation in Western Europe, it would be false--not to
say insulting--to brand as Communists or Communist sym-
pathizers the legion of individuals of good will who
are haunted by the specter of nuclear incineration and
are caught up in the turmoil that rages about the
deployment of nuclear missiles in their backyards, as
it were. Soviet missiles, perhaps because of the distant venues in which they are housed, do not appear as
threatening as U.S. weapons slated for nearby loca-
tions, although the mission of U.S. weapons is to protect the security of Western Europe. The immediacy of
the inherent threat that emanates from the known destructive potential of these weapons, their felt--or
rather their anticipated--presence must in large part
account for the emotionality that has seized significant segments of the population in the Federal Republic
of Germany and other European countries.

For their part, the protagonists of LRTNF, particularly in the United States, have also contributed
to the creation of an atmosphere of panic by nurturing
and popularizing a perception of overwhelming Soviet
superiority. This is an intrinsically dangerous exercise, akin, perhaps, to clearing a crowded theater by
shouting, "Fire!" There must be other, less dramatic
ways of trying to mobilize public opinion than by
spreading tales of horror, which in fact could induce
the opposite of what they intend, either by instilling
a sense of abject resignation in the face of crushing
Soviet superiority or, alternatively, by raising doubt
about the veracity of claims which appear exaggerated
and remain unconvincingly substantiated.

The avowed intention of the U.S. government to
share with West European governments and to release to
the public a mass of intelligence data authenticating
its claims of an awesome Soviet military buildup is a
step in the right direction. The distribution of information, however, must be carried out with restraint
and discernment and must not take on the proportions of
a mind-numbing stampede.[13]

The long-delayed beginning of U.S.-Soviet negotia-
tions--a process which is due to unfold before our eyes
in the nearest future--might also help to stem feelings of distrust in the good faith of the American

government.[14]   Much   depends   on the course   of   the
negotiations,   and expectations of an early   resolution
of the Soviet-American contretemps would be optimistic.
        Neither power may be in a hurry to get on with the
substance of the talks.   Paul Nitze's selection as the
chief American negotiator guarantees a hard-bitten,
skeptical approach,   for he harbors bitter memories of
his earlier participation in arms control   discussions
with   the Russians.   The Soviet representative may   be
under   instructions to engage in dilatory   tactics,   at
least   pending an assessment by Soviet   authorities   of
how promising the defeat of the Doppelbeschluss appears
to   be   at   the hands of the anti-nuclear   movement   in
Western   Europe.   The   agenda itself is likely   to   be
troublesome.   Will the Soviet Union in effect   attempt
to   exploit these negotiations to sustain the   momentum
of   anti-nuclear agitation?   To this end,   the   Soviet
Union   could   set   conditions which the   United   States
could   not accept as a basis for talks and thus try   to
put   the   onus on the Reagan administration   for   being
"uncooperative."   And   what about the   United   States?
Will   it confront the Soviet Union with   political   demands which the Kremlin could not honor without seeming
to retreat from firm positions it has taken on a number
of international problems?
        While   the issue of middle-range nuclear   missiles
is of surpassing importance, particularly to Europeans,
it   is not the only one over which the superpowers   are
at odds with each other.   Tensions between them are not
likely to abate quickly, even if progress is registered
toward   the resolution of the LRTNF/SS-20   controversy.
There   is   no denying that such progress would help   to
calm the international climate and assuage some of   the
worst fears of European public opinion.   But Europeans
generally   will feel uneasy as long as the   superpowers
remain in an essentially confrontational posture.
        Unfortunately,   given   the prevailing mood in   Eu-
rope, the United States may bear the brunt of the blame
if   little or no progress is registered in the   middle-
range   missile   negotiations and tensions   between   the
superpowers   remain at a high level.   The Soviet Union
has   skillfully   maneuvered itself into a   position   of
greater   credibility.   Its intentions and motives   are
less suspect and certainly less rigorously   scrutinized
by many Europeans.   Brezhnev's blandishments often seem
accepted at face value.   The bona fides of the American
government--for   example,   in repeatedly affirming   its
intentions   to open negotiations with the Soviet   Union
before   the   end   of 1981--are seldom   given   the   same
currency.
        It is questionable if doubts about American inten-
tions   will   soon   be totally dissipated and   a   proper
context for judging U.S.   policies,   restored.   These
doubts, though more prevalent now than in the past, are

not of contemporary origin. They run the gamut from suspicions about American steadfastness in defending its allies to fear of the propensity the United States might have to fight a war on European soil that endangers the survival of European nations. The persistence of such doubts can be attributed to immutable objective factors as much as to subjective aspects of European-American relations.

The geostrategic structure of the alliance is simply lopsided and has always been so. In the past, when the United States was far and away the strongest power, this did not seem to matter. Present conditions differ markedly from those of bygone years. Consequently, the existing asymmetry is more evident, and the policies of the member states of the alliance are more difficult to coordinate. The physical detachment of the chief guarantor from its allies evokes heightened feelings of apprehension, especially in countries that feel particularly dependent because they do not possess nuclear weapons. The Federal Republic is in the most precarious position because its exposed geographic location renders it exceptionally vulnerable, and the burden of its historic legacy, which includes the division of Germany (as it existed before Hitler's territorial conquests) into two entities, weighs heavily upon it.

It is problematic if any juggling of the location of American nuclear forces would suffice to allay suspicions and doubts about America's role in helping to shape the destiny of Europe. To be sure, corresponding suspicions and apprehensions about the policies of European governments and the trends in European public opinion abound in the United States.

The alliance suffers from a crisis of confidence, which is to some extent of its own making. There are no patent medicine remedies to help surmount this crisis. But surmounted it has to be. For nothing, not even the outside threat of the Soviet Union, can be as detrimental to the welfare of the alliance as a lack of unity among its members.

Policy decisions may have to be reviewed and revised as dictated by necessity. The Doppelbeschluss is no exception. It should be subjected to searching scrutiny to determine if it needs to be altered. Fear of losing credibility in the event a recent decision is adapted to new conditions cannot be the guiding principle of decision making in the alliance. Such adaptations, of course, exclude capitulation to outside pressure. But clinging stubbornly to a decision, the implementation of which may in the long run be prevented by massive popular opposition, would have even more deleterious political consequences than the appearance of indecisiveness. This is not to advocate jettisoning the Doppelbeschluss, which rests on solid premises, but to urge that the rationale for its provisions be more convincingly substantiated, more lucidly explained, and placed in the context of a comprehensive strategic framework that may command greater public acceptance.

Given the prevailing democratic order in Western societies, public opinion exercises a decisive influence on political outcomes. Polarization of the body politic--or, still worse, violent public strife--already threatens to tear asunder stable political structures and further endanger the stability of the alliance. Perpetuation of such destructive tendencies in the political life of their countries must be intolerable for NATO governments. They must seek to cement relations with significant portions of the population who tend to be basically responsible and constructive, build consensus in support of common alliance policies by dealing with the people forthrightly, and show compassion and understanding for people's anxieties.

Confidence building within the alliance is the order of the day. Improved Atlantic cooperation is of necessity a resultant of collective cooperative efforts by all members of the alliance. There must be reciprocity among them in fostering cooperation. Still, the impetus must come in the first place from the United States as the leading power.

The style and substance of leadership exercised by the United States has to be adapted to present-day realities and requirements. Muscle-flexing by the United States might well be tempered by a display of greater sensitivity for the national interests, ambitions, fears, and even idiosyncracies of other countries, which should be susceptible to accommodation within the alliance framework. Utterances to the effect that the defense decisions of the United States cannot be made in Europe have a strong jingoistic tinge and reflect a certain myopia concerning alliance relations, especially if the decisions pertain to issues that vitally affect the security of the European members of the alliance.

Extensive programs of arms procurement requiring the commitment of stupendous monetary resources are in themselves not convincing. They need to be buttressed by efforts to secure an adequate manpower base for the U.S. military establishment, enabling it to carry out the country's self-assumed global responsibilities. Without conscription, the United States will not lightly persuade either friend or adversary that its mammoth rearmament program is not basically a sham.

Procurement of weapons systems would also gain in credibility if it did not project an image of helter-skelter decisions made without reference to a cogent, comprehensive strategy and designed to meet the exacting military and political requirements of the present era.

Elaboration of strategic concepts adequate to the task of accommodating the desideratum of war avoidance (through deterrence and negotiations) has been long overdue. The difficulties attendant upon the elaboration of such concepts are formidable--not in the least because they rest on the tenuous, if unavoidable, precept of cooperative crisis management between adversaries. War avoidance as a supreme strategic objective runs counter to the teachings of classical military strategy, and it is thus likely to be resisted by military, if not by political, leaders. Neither superpower has yet shown an inclination to reconcile itself to the restraints inherent in cooperative crisis management. The failure of the first halting steps made in this direction in the 1970s bears testimony to the reluctance of both to abide by the dictates of this new and unfamiliar initiative. The USSR has not yet divested itself of the ideological fetters which hold it hostage to a conflict-winning orientation (Kto kogo),[15] and the United States has been loath to abandon its self-image as the leading power in the world. The psychological hazards impeding the necessary attitudinal change on the part of both superpowers are not trifling. Yet the alternative is stark--it confronts mankind with the grim prospect of global holocaust.

The Fate of Poland: Dilemma for the West
February 1982

Throughout the centuries and at historic junctures, the fate of Poland and the destiny of Europe have frequently been intertwined. It was so in 1939-- it appears so today. Then, sluggish and ill-prepared Western governments, which had abjectly countenanced a series of aggressive ventures by Hitler's Third Reich, finally aroused themselves from their moral torpor and resisted the latest and most blatant act of Nazi aggression--unprovoked military attack on Poland. World War II began. Now, circumstances are somewhat different. War is not imminent. But the Polish crisis does have far-reaching international implications, no matter how vehemently Moscow and Warsaw argue that it is purely a domestic affair of the Poles in which the West should not meddle. The West's response to the crisis is crucial; it could be fateful. It will decisively influence the course of East-West relations for some time to come.

An analysis of the contemporary events we confront should be cast in a broad historic context. The Polish

crisis of today is in large measure a consequence of
the unfinished legacy of World War II. Hitler's assault on Poland took place in overt collusion with
Stalin, and the Soviet Union became a direct beneficiary of the renewed partition of Poland. The territory seized by Stalin in 1939 (and temporarily lost by
him during the war) was reconquered in the westward
sweep of the Red Army and was never again relinquished.
    In the wake of the war which started in Poland in
1939 and ended in Berlin nearly six years later, the
face of Europe was drastically changed. New power
arrangements emerged. They were enshrined in agreement
concluded by the Big Three--Roosevelt, Churchill, and
Stalin--at the Black Sea resort of Yalta on the Crimean
coast in February 1945. "Yalta" has since served as a
convenient shorthand reference to the division of Europe into two spheres of influence, with special reference to the predominance of the Soviet Union in Eastern
Europe.
    The legacy of Yalta has burdened international
relations in Europe for nearly four decades, and it
still does. This is so because the Soviet Union considers its sphere of influence a privileged sanctuary
and brooks no outside interference in it. During the
tedious years of the cold war the strictures imposed by
the Soviet Union caused fewer problems than in the more
recent period. Europe was divided into two hostile
camps. The "captive nations" of Eastern Europe were
confined behind an "Iron Curtain." Ultimately, both
sides considered this condition untenable. Policies of
greater accommodation and cooperation spelled the cold
war in the late sixties and early seventies. Their
intent was to open up clogged channels of interaction
and overcome the worst effects of the division of
Europe. The centerpiece of these policies was the
Helsinki agreement, signed in August 1975 by thirty-
three European and two North American powers. A new
proper noun entered the vocabulary of international
relations--Helsinki. It did not consign Yalta to
oblivion; in a sense, however, that is what it was
intended to accomplish, at least in the view of the
Western powers.
    The Soviet Union saw the Helsinki agreement as a
sort of surrogate peace treaty, ratifying the inviolability of the postwar frontiers in Europe (which the
Soviet Union interpreted as sanctifying Soviet territorial conquests and the status quo in Eastern Europe)
and setting the stage for a gradual erosion of the
Western powers' will to face up to the threat of armed
conflict on the continent.
    The Western powers, in turn, expected that the
Helsinki agreement would promote processes of expanded
political and trade relations and encourage the adoption of an acceptable international standard of human

*Helsinki, which codified Yalta, and detente
are the West's hopes to loosen the grip on
Eastern Europe.*

rights in the East.   Altogether, these processes would
lead to a reduction of tensions and mutual suspicions.
Confidence building would be conducive to arms control,
and that would diminish the threat of armed conflict.
It was their hope that gradual processes of multilateral interaction in the long run would tame the
Communist regimes, particularly the Soviet, so that
peaceful coexistence would become a permanent, meaningful reality resting on solid foundations.   In other
words, the effects of Yalta would at last be miti-
gated without threatening the security of the Soviet
Union.
     These hopes were based on tenuous premises and
probably failed to take into account a built-in contra-
diction in the detente process, as the Western powers
envisaged it.   To wit--to be successful, detente must
not threaten the stability of any regime.   In fact, the
mutual stability of states belonging to adversary alliances is a precondition for confidence building. Yet
detente is principally predicated on change. Change is
potentially destabilizing, and destabilization is bound
to be viewed by the Soviet Union and most of the East
European Communist regimes as threatening.   They are
very defensive about the viability of their political,
social, and economic structures and are unwilling to
risk their disestablishment as a consequence of a growing interdependence with Western democratic systems.
Detente is thus possessed of a strongly self-limiting
quality, if it is not self-invalidating.
     This is not to say that detente has not produced
what appear to be positive results in Europe. For many
Europeans, it is the only condition of existence. The
alternative--another cold war in whatever incarnation--
holds out no prospect whatever. It is a dead end. For
some, like the West Germans, it is literally a blank
wall against which they would butt and bloody their
heads in vain.
     But detente has in fact promoted instability in
both alliance systems, albeit of a different nature.
In the West, detente has driven Western Europe and
America apart from each other.   The United States has
reaped fewer tangible benefits from it and has been
more alarmed by the palpable evidence of Soviet aggressive behavior on a global scale.   In the East, detente
has helped to unleash internal trends in Communist
regimes, which in Poland gave rise to the explosive
developments of the past year-and-a-half.
     The Polish process of renewal, starting in August
1980, was fundamentally a challenge to the structure
which was created at Yalta.   It threatened not just to
undermine that structure, but to replace it by a new
one.   At least the Soviet Union appears to have interpreted it in this light.   Hence, the crackdown on
Solidarnosc, the nationwide trade union movement which

Detente promoted instability not only in both alliances -- wedge between US and European allies -- exacerbated internal dissent in the East.

108

became the institutional embodiment of national renewal.

The events of the past year-and-a-half up to the
imposition of martial law on December 13, 1981 (a state
of war between the Polish authorities and the people)
bespoke a search--revolutionary in scope but peaceful
in character--for new institutional and political power
relations and new economic structures, consonant with
the country's needs and the people's aspirations. It
is remarkable how little violence accompanied the Polish renewal, and such violence as did occur was minor.
There were no bloody clashes between workers and the
police. Above all, there were no fatal injuries, although some dozens of militiamen were roughed up here
and there, and there was one incident (an attempted
provocation by the police in the city of Bydgosc) which
resulted in bodily harm to several trade union
leaders.

This peaceful search did not threaten to encroach
on Poland's international obligations (its membership
in the Warsaw Pact and Comecon), and thus it did not
endanger Soviet security interests in Europe, as we
would tend to define these. The Soviet definition
tends to be more stringent. It includes a strict interpretation of the type of domestic system or order to
which the member states of the alliance must adhere.
This severely restricts the possibilities of systemic
change and inhibits the attainment of national self-
determination.

For decades, the Soviet Union has tolerated certain aberrations from the norm in Poland (a predominantly private agricultural economy and the Catholic Church which, though not free until the renewal,
nevertheless freely catered to the spiritual needs of
the people and did have influence). During the process
of renewal itself, the Soviet Union acted with restraint for a considerable time, although it exerted
unrelenting pressure on the hapless Communist party to
stem the tide of renewal. In the end, Soviet patience
wore thin, and the results are well known.

It is ridiculous to pretend that the Polish Communist military acted entirely on its own in declaring
martial law. It would not have dared to do so for fear
that the Soviet Union, which has a healthy respect for
the uses of military power, might misconstrue the purposes of a nationwide deployment of Polish military
units. The Soviet Union preferred this method to quell
the process of renewal and to stop a process of anar-
chization that did threaten to engulf the country in
chaos (if not in civil war), because a Warsaw Pact
invasion on the model of Czechoslovakia would have
probably encountered massive resistance in Poland.
Soviet restraint was also dictated by an ongoing effort
to forestall the deployment of U.S. LRTNF in Europe

and, to this end, to mobilize anti-nuclear sentiment among West European pacifists and other groups. Overt aggression against Poland would have made it more difficult, if not impossible, to continue fostering anti-nuclear agitation in Europe. It would have thus undermined a high priority Soviet foreign policy objective. Even now there is evidence that Western anti-nuclear forces have been adversely affected by the declaration of martial law in Poland. The Soviet government has tried to counter this loss of momentum and enthusiasm among the anti-nuclear forces by hinting that it would be prepared to make much larger unilateral cuts in its arsenal of Euromissiles than it had previously indicated.

Be that as it may, the method of Soviet intervention is strikingly different from that employed in Hungary in 1956 and in Czechoslovakia in 1968. The limits of tolerance of the Soviet Union, although it took longer to arrive at them, have not substantially changed. The bottom line is to prevent the pluralization of political power, the introduction of genuine freedom of expression and assembly, and the decentralization of economic controls through the introduction of industrial self-management.

The future of Poland is uncertain and bleak. If the martial law regime should not be able to restore order, the Soviet Union would not hesitate to intervene, whatever the cost of intervention might be in bloodshed and lost opportunities in Western Europe. But it now seems that the Polish military under General Wojciech Jaruzelski is quite capable of maintaining itself indefinitely, if necessary, with a very firm hand. Ultimately, the Communist party, now in shambles, may be rebuilt. It happened in Hungary, where the party was totally smashed during the revolution. The way things seem to be going now, Solidarnosc, if it is allowed to reconstitute itself, will be but a hollow shell, a caricature of its former robust self.[16] Human rights, and intellectual and artistic freedoms are well on the way to being eradicated. A massive purge of journalists is just one case in point about which we have reliable information.

The Church's wings have also been effectively clipped. Its condemnation of martial law; its demands for negotiations between the military and the trade unions; its pleas for the release of Lech Walesa (the trade union leader from Gdansk catapulted to national stature, and whom the authorities placed under house arrest when martial law was imposed) have fallen on deaf ears. These demands did not even elicit a rebuttal. Since the Church cannot in good conscience call on the people to rise in arms against the military, it must in fact counsel acquiescence in the state of affairs, in order to avoid loss of life and minimize

Church can't in good conscience call for an uprising or even call on its members to resist the gov't because of the great risks it would entail to the economy,

acute physical suffering. At most, it can urge passive resistance, and that is likely to develop on a large scale. Unfortunately, passive resistance (that is, failure to cooperate with the authorities) will help to compound the country's enormous, almost insurmountable economic difficulties--a staggering hard currency indebtedness from which the country may not be able to extricate itself for decades, if at all, and shortages of every imaginable kind (including foodstuffs, clothes, durable goods, housing, and heavy industrial products).[17] Even before the declaration of martial law, it was estimated that economic recovery would take at a minimum three to five years, and the housing shortage--one of the most acute sources of popular frustration--could not be alleviated for up to ten years. Two million applicants for housing have been waiting for new quarters for ten years. Imagine the queue some years from now.

Clearly, the population will have to endure incredible privation. Will they be able to bear it? How will they react? But apart from affecting the Polish people, the baneful effects of the Polish economic disaster will make themselves felt internationally. The Soviet Union and its East European allies will bear the brunt of these effects. There will be far-reaching consequences for the living standards of their people and for the very viability of their economic systems. In the competition between East and West, in which the economic disabilities of the Communist systems have already been glaringly exposed, the East is bound to be further disadvantaged. In this sense, the Polish events may indeed be noted by historians one day as the beginning of the disintegration of Soviet-type socialist systems. But one must guard against making apocalyptic predictions.

The West, which has been impotent in the face of a crackdown on the Polish renewal and will probably not be able to help save any vestige of it, will, of course, have future opportunities to bring its influence to bear on developments in Poland, throughout Eastern Europe, and in the Soviet Union.

To date, the manner in which the Western alliance as a whole, and individual members of the alliance separately, reacted to the declaration of martial law and to the ensuing events in Poland has revealed a lack of coordination which may not be too surprising, under the circumstances. More disturbing is that a wide divergence of attitudes bordering on discord among the allies has also been revealed.

Lack of coordination may be attributed to a dismal intelligence and planning failure. The allies geared up to respond to a Soviet invasion which never took place and were unprepared to cope with another contingency. The declaration of martial law took them by

Soviet Union and others of the bloc will also bear the burden to get Poland on its feet again

surprise. They needed time to develop a response to a
much more difficult fait accompli, because indirect
aggression on the part of the Soviet Union (provided
they all agreed on that point) cannot be satisfactorily substantiated, although circumstantial evidence may abound and cold logic would suggest that
what took place was a classical case of indirect aggression.

I do not want to speculate about the reasons for
the failure to anticipate something other than Soviet
armed assault. In the absence of a coordinated alliance position, one had to be developed in haste and
actually was, in rather short order. On January 11,
1982, a little less than a full month after martial law
had been imposed, the NATO foreign ministers met in
special session and issued a sixteen-point declaration
which specified three conditions for a return to normal
relations with Poland: an end to martial law; the
release of detainees; and the resumption of talks between the state, the Church, and the trade unions.
Otherwise, sanctions were threatened. Although the
declaration asserted that "the Soviet Union has no
right to determine the political and social development of Poland," it invoked no sanctions against
the Soviet Union and gave each member statewide latitude to "identify appropriate national possibilities
for action . . . within its own situation and legisla-
tion."[18]

Not surprisingly, the declaration was totally
ineffectual in inducing Polish authorities to change
the course on which they had embarked. It constituted
no more than a slap on the wrist of the Soviet Union
and allowed each country to do (or not do) whatever it
wanted. It was a face-saving gesture, although hardly
a respectable one, which accomplished little beyond
exacerbating the war of invectives between East and
West.

It is difficult to escape the conclusion that
martial law in Poland precipitated another crisis in
the Western alliance, which is already badly divided
over the issue of LRTNF and has barely recovered--if at
all--from the disarray into which it was thrust by the
Soviet invasion of Afghanistan. The basic source of
these recurring crises, which now threaten to tear the
alliance asunder, rests in the members' divergent assessments of the Soviet threat and the varying conclusions they draw how they should deal with the Soviet
Union. In addition, there are differences in diplomatic style among the countries and in the personalities of their leaders. Stylistic and personality differences by themselves would be relatively unimportant,
but they tend to acquire increased significance when
they are added to basic policy disagreements. Then
they act as irritants of major proportions.

Our European allies in general, but the West Germans in particular, are at odds with our preoccupation with the Soviet military threat and our reluctance to attend to the economic problems troubling the alliance. Their list of grievances is long, as is ours; for we believe that they do not want to carry their share of the burden for the common defense and are misguided in believing that good faith interaction with the Soviet Union is possible. The West Germans have come under special suspicion for being downright neutralists, standing or trying to stand between the two camps rather than being steadfast members of the Western alliance.

President Reagan's righteous expressions of moral outrage at the brutal suppression of the Polish people[19] (expressions which are in keeping with his own impulsive character and his deep convictions and which are consistent with the general orientation of the vast majority of his countrymen) tend to be the subject of derision, if not of cynical disbelief, in Europe. This is so because the list of sanctions imposed by the president on Poland and the Soviet Union seems puny. Missing among them is the only sanction which might be effective--an embargo on grain sales-- which at the same time would hurt the American farmer and thus harm the American economy.[20]

West Germany's failure to register any outrage whatever at the imposition of martial law in Warsaw is taken in America as a sign of moral turpitude and evidence of how low the Germans have sunk in their efforts to appease the Soviet Union.[21] There is little inclination in the United States to desist from maligning the Germans, who are in the most sensitive and vulnerable position among all NATO allies, not only and not even primarily because of their trade relations with the East, but for many other reasons. Among these are the vulnerability of Berlin; the intricate contacts with East Germany, which impose on the West German authorities a moral responsibility not to aggravate the conditions of the East German population and add to the hardships that a large number of West Germans would have to endure (because they have relatives and friends in East Germany); and the sense of guilt still felt by many Germans for the atrocities perpetrated on Poles during World War II. It would not behoove the Germans to interfere in the internal affairs of Poland.

The French, of course, are never reluctant to detect nefarious motives in West Germany's dealings with East Germany and the Soviet Union. The specter of Rapallo is easily revived in Paris.

Yet the French themselves are not unambiguous in their stance toward the Polish crisis. In France, as in other European countries, policies toward the Soviet Union are intimately related to domestic political

imperatives. In this instance, the uneasy alliance of
Socialists and Communists in France creates a particularly intriguing situation. In West Germany, of
course, the conservative opposition parties are occasionally driven to excessively harsh criticism of the
social-liberal government, which they would like to
replace at the earliest opportunity. The Polish crisis
is thus divisive in many ways--internationally and
nationally.

A basic Western strategy that would yield optimum
results is not easily arrived at. Experience with
sanctions has been relatively discouraging. To impose
them as mere expressions of displeasure is futile (in
the view of many Europeans, "immature"), yet not to
impose them conveys the impression of moral indifference ("business as usual"). Should the Soviet
Union be punished (disciplined) for its misdeeds? Most
Europeans cringe at the concept of punishment in international relations. But what is the alternative to
sanctions or punishment--incentives? What sorts of
incentives would be effective, and effective in accom-
plishing what?

The West appears to have economic leverage on the
East--trade, but especially loans--which it could use
either in the form of sanctions or of incentives. The
use of this leverage is complicated, because Western
countries have different economic interests of their
own and because private enterprise is heavily involved,
as in the hard currency loans to Poland. The problems
now attendant upon the liquidation of the Polish debt
($26 billion or more, $16 billion of it owed to private
institutions), the terms of servicing outstanding
loans, and the question of new loans probably overtax
the capabilities of the commercial banks because of the
magnitude and complexity of the financial obligations
involved and the circumstances of the debtor. This is
not a matter of traditional financial policies that can
be resolved within the framework of familiar banking
practices, but a matter of state, in which private
enterprise must seek the cooperation and guidance of
government.

Judging by the plethora of advice given from the
sidelines, there is no dearth of ingenious schemes that
could be explored, but the advice from the sidelines is
as confused and contradictory as are the policies of
the governments. Former Secretary of State Henry
Kissinger berates President Reagan for not suspending
arms talks with the Soviet Union. Felix G. Rohatyn,
senior partner of Lazard Freres, suggests that we
should let Poland go broke.[22] And there are others
who think that we could use monetary incentives to
wring concessions from the Poles and their masters.

I am not in possession of any superior wisdom and
do not purport to know what set or sets of policies

114

would be most effective. One thought occurs. Would it
be possible to devise a trade-off between economic
incentives the West would offer the Soviet Union for a
commensurate reduction of the Soviet Union's military
might?
        The burden of Yalta still weighs upon us.   In his
1982 New Year's message, President François Mitterand
of France spoke directly to the Polish situation and
said ruefully, "Anything which would permit us to escape from Yalta would be good, on condition that we
never confuse our wishes with the reality of the
present day." Henry Kissinger, in his recent attack on
the foreign policy of the Reagan administration (an
attack provoked by the Polish crisis), reminds us of
the other side of the coin, that the Yalta agreement
also called for free elections in Poland.
        Instead of engaging in mutual recrimination, it
might be more prudent if the West sought to close ranks
and develop common policies that would help to redeem
our past shortcomings, omissions, or sense of guilt.
None of the Western powers has a clear track record;
none is in a position to point a finger at the other.
        If we allow the Polish crisis to weaken still fur-
ther the already frayed fabric of the Western alliance,
we would be doing a disservice to ourselves and to the
Polish people.   Only the Soviet Union would benefit.
If we cannot actively help the Polish people to gain
their freedom--and it is clear that our opportunities
to do so are severely constrained--we should at least
not let the Soviet Union derive advantages from a
situation that should by all odds be an unmitigated
disaster for it.

NOTES

        1. North Atlantic Assembly, Sub-Committee on De-
tente, Detente Results and Prospects (Brussels, 1979).
        The North Atlantic Assembly is the inter-
parliamentary body of member states of the North Atlantic alliance.   It is composed of 172 members who are
nominated by the respective national legislatures. The
assembly provides a forum where West European and
North American parliamentarians meet regularly to analyze, discuss, and voice their opinion on alliance
issues and developments, and it acts as a link between
NATO authorities and the legislators of the member
states.
        2. The fears expressed about the unwillingness of
the Soviet Union to negotiate about the reduction of
middle-range nuclear missiles proved to be exaggerated.
After a period of about six months, Leonid I. Brezhnev
allowed himself to be persuaded by Helmut Schmidt (on
the occasion of the West German chancellor's official

visit in Moscow in late June and early July 1980) to agree that preliminary discussions on limiting middle-range systems could begin. Brezhnev did take the position, however, that U.S. forward-based systems (FBS) should be drawn into the negotiations and stated that no agreement or treaty on LRTNF could be implemented before SALT II was ratified.

3. According to a report issued by the Special Committee on Nuclear Weapons in Europe of the North Atlantic Assembly:

> European observers and officials alike expressed the almost unanimous view that the non-ratification of SALT II had had a profound effect on public opinion in Europe. It had been a major factor in the growth of opposition to the NATO [LRTNF] decision [taken in December 1979] and the rise of the anti-nuclear movements.

North Atlantic Assembly, Special Committee on Nuclear Weapons, Interim Report (Brussels, November 1982), 25.

4. For the text of the communique issued following the special meeting of the foreign and defense ministers of NATO, see North Atlantic Treaty Organization, NATO Handbook (Brussels: NATO Information Service, August 1980), 68-70.

5. Radomir Bogdanov, deputy director of the Institute of U.S. and Canadian Studies of the Soviet Academy of Sciences, makes an interesting point in a recent article that echoes sentiments uttered by some West Europeans: "All European cities are separated from one another by a distance of not more than the range of a two-kiloton nuclear bomb." Radomir Bogdanov, "The Truth about Euromissiles," Moscow News, no. 38 (1981).

6. Theo Sommer, "Die Euro-Gleichung," Die Zeit, April 24, 1981.

7. Der Bundesminister der Verteidigung, Die Nuklearen Mittelstreckenwaffen, Modernisierung und Rüstungskontrolle: Texte, Materialen und Argumente zum Beschluss der NATO vom 12 Dezember 1979 (Bonn: Bundesminister der Verteidigung, Planungsstab, April 22, 1980).

8. Confusion about numbers is compounded if one notes the respective claims made by the United States and the USSR. In an interview he gave the West German weekly Der Spiegel prior to his visit to the Federal Republic of Germany in November 1981, Leonid Brezhnev asserted that a rough balance existed between NATO and the Warsaw Pact in medium-range nuclear delivery systems in Europe. According to Brezhnev, the NATO countries had 986 nuclear delivery systems (including missiles and aircraft) and the Soviet Union possessed 975. These figures have not been revised since then by Soviet spokesmen, although deployment of SS-20s continued after 1981. For a Soviet English language text

of the Brezhnev interview, see Moscow News, Supplement
to issue no. 45 (1981).

The United States, for its part, credits NATO with
395 delivery systems and the Soviet Union with 1,920.
As far as warheads are concerned, the United States
claims that NATO disposes over 707 against 3,870 for
the Soviet Union. For U.S. estimates of delivery systems and warheads, see Donald R. Cotter, James H.
Hansen, and Kirk McConnell, The Nuclear "Balance" in
Europe: Status, Trends, Implications, USSI Report 83-1
(Cambridge: United States Strategic Institute, 1983).

Not surprisingly, the Soviet figures show NATO in
the lead with 1,481 warheads against the Soviet Union's
975. (The Soviet Union does not acknowledge multiple
warheads on its missiles and a carrying capacity of
more than one single warhead "bomb" per aircraft.)

9. The International Institute for Strategic Stud-
ies lists three variants of the SS-20:
   Mod. 1 with one warhead of 1.5 megatons and
   a range of 5,000 kilometers
   Mod. 2 with three warheads of 150 kilotons
   each and a range of 5,000 kilometers
   Mod. 3 with one warhead of 50 kilotons and
   a range of 7,400 kilometers
International Institute for Strategic Studies, The
Military Balance, 1982-1983 (London, 1982), 113.

10. Some people in Europe, particularly in the
Federal Republic of Germany, would acquiesce in a cer-
tain degree of Soviet superiority even if the United
States had zero missiles, provided that the number of
Soviet missiles ranged between 50 and 75.

President Reagan announced the U.S. position on
November 18, 1981, which called for a "zero solution,"
that is, zero missiles on the American side in exchange
for zero missiles on the Soviet side. The United
States would not deploy if the Soviet Union agreed to
destroy all its medium-range missiles aimed at Europe.
On March 31, 1983, the president provisionally relented
from this severe position by substituting an interim
solution in its place. This called for reductions by
the Soviet Union to an equal level with the United
States. Under the provisions of the interim solution,
the United States would proceed to deploy, but not the
full complement of 572 launchers. The number of U.S.
weapons to be deployed would be determined by the level
to which the Soviet Union was willing to reduce. At
the same time, the president listed "standards of fairness" to which the Soviet Union would have to adhere.
The president's interim solution was no more acceptable
to the Russians than was his zero solution. Both asked
the Soviet Union to dismantle forces in being, against
the non-deployment of weapons that did not yet exist.

The Soviet Union, for its part, announced modifications in its position in a series of public

statements. On December 21, 1982, Yuri Andropov indicated that the Soviet Union "would be prepared to reduce its medium-range missiles in Europe to match the number of French and British missiles, that is, 162." Pravda, December 22, 1981. On May 3, 1983, Andropov declared that his country would undertake reductions on the basis of reciprocity with NATO and would agree to counting warheads as units of reduction. Pravda, May 4, 1983.

The snag in the warhead count may be that the Soviet Union attributes to NATO a lead of roughly one-and-a-half to one in medium-range warheads. In addition, Andropov's proposal of May 3 encompassed the French and British nuclear forces (which the president in his "standards of fairness" had specifically excluded from INF negotiations); he pointedly referred to a European balance without mentioning Asia (the president had stated that an agreement must not shift the [nuclear] threat from Europe to Asia); and he remained silent on the question of verifiability (the president had insisted that an agreement must be effectively verifiable).

Judging by their public postures at the end of the summer of 1983 (just before the beginning of the final round of INF talks in Geneva on September 6), the superpowers were not likely to compose their differences before the end of the year when, in the absence of an agreement, deployment of U.S. medium-range missiles in Europe would begin.

11. Negotiations opened in Geneva on November 30, 1981. The Reagan administration dropped the acronym LRTNF and substituted intermediate-range nuclear force (INF) in its place.

12. President Carter actually initiated preliminary talks in October 1980, in the waning moments of the presidential campaign. These were suspended shortly after they had begun.

13. In September 1981, the U.S. Department of Defense released a report of nearly 100 pages under the title Soviet Military Power. (A second edition of this report was issued in March 1983.) The avowed purpose of the 1981 version was "to make available to people everywhere a factual report on the magnitude of the Soviet military buildup and the changing character of Soviet military objectives." In the preface to the 1983 edition, Secretary of Defense Caspar W. Weinberger stated that "the updated facts . . . leave no doubt as to the USSR's dedication to achieving military superiority in all fields." In his words, "It is our duty to have a full awareness of Soviet military growth, modernization, and capabilities, and to shape our defense forces and our deterrent capabilities accordingly."

It is doubtful if this particular publication is well-suited to communicate the concerns of the Pentagon to a large audience. For one thing, the format of the report is awkward. Its large size, the heavy glossy paper on which it is printed, and the high cost for which it can be purchased from the Government Printing Office ($6) do not make it an item with mass appeal, especially abroad. For another thing, the report tries too hard to prove its point and does so without presenting readily discernible, credible, and convincing evidence. There are too many adjectives in the text, which in addition is often too general (undoubtedly to mask intelligence data or the sources of intelligence information). Supporting illustrations consist of file photos of Soviet military equipment and artist's conceptions of Soviet armaments and installations.

14. As indicated above in footnote 11, negotiations began in Geneva on November 30, 1981.

15. The expression is V.I. Lenin's. In English translation it literally means, "Who, whom." It connotes Lenin's conception of politics as a struggle for survival, both in the national and international context.

16. As part of a series of elaborate measures which the Polish authorities took in preparation of the formal lifting of martial law, the Sejm (Parliament) explicitly outlawed Solidarnosc on October 8, 1982, and forbade the reconstitution of this organization in any guise.

17. For an excellent summary analysis of economic conditions in Poland at the beginning of 1981, Polish indebtedness to the West, and Poland's economic prospects, see Heinrich Machowski, Die Verschuldung der Volksrepublik Polen gegenüber dem Westen, Vierteljahrshefte zur Wirtschaftsforschung (Berlin: Deutsches Institut für Wirtschaftsforschung, 1981) 1:53-64.

18. North Atlantic Treaty Organization, Press Release M-1(82)1 (Brussels: NATO Press Service, January 11, 1982).

19. Radio and TV address of President Ronald Reagan, December 23, 1981. New York Times, December 24, 1981.

20. Actually, on December 29, 1981, the president announced a postponement of American-Soviet negotiations about a new long-term grain agreement. New York Times, December 30, 1981.

21. See, for example, comments by Rowland Evans and Robert Novak, "Warning Schmidt Quietly"; also, "An Atlantic Gap Widens," editorial from the Washington Post; both printed in the International Herald Tribune, January 4, 1982.

22. Felix G. Rohatyn, "We Should Let Poland Go Broke," San Francisco Chronicle, January 24, 1982, This World Supplement, 27.

5
A Look into the 1980s

The two parts of this chapter were completed in July and September 1982, respectively. They summarize trends and project developments in NATO and in Western Europe, particularly in the Federal Republic of Germany. Neither part focuses specifically on military issues, although the Soviet-American confrontation over middle-range nuclear forces has in the recent past agitated European publics to an extraordinary degree. At times it has seemed as if other aspects of East-West relations had been nearly erased from public consciousness. My concerns center on the political and psychological cohesiveness of the transatlantic alliance and the community of Western states in Europe.

In reviewing trends that are likely to have an impact on Western political stability, I take account of the rise of anti-nuclear sentiment in Europe, the structure and activities of the peace movement, and the exertions of the Soviet Union to exploit to its advantage the desire for peace in Western Europe. I also explore a range of economic and social problems with which advanced industrial societies (primarily, but not exclusively, in Western Europe) have to contend.

While the contents of this chapter are oriented toward the future, they do not contain bold predictions nor do they prescribe panaceas. At most, they offer prudent estimates about the configuration of problems which might be anticipated by the Western countries in their search for appropriate means to retain mastery over their collective and individual destinies.

In the course of a year since the essays in this chapter were written, significant changes have taken place in the national leadership of the Federal Republic of Germany and of the Soviet Union.

In the Federal Republic, a change of government (which was imminent) occurred on October 4, 1982. Helmut Kohl, the leader of the conservative Christian Democratic Union (CDU), replaced the Social Democrat Helmut Schmidt as chancellor. This change was

119

confirmed in parliamentary elections held on March 6, 1983. On this occasion, the Greens also gained representation in the Bundestag for the first time, contributing to the greater complexity of the West German political scene. The economy, meanwhile, has so far not registered the upturn hoped for under the new government, by the majority of the population.

In the Soviet Union, Leonid I. Brezhnev died on November 10, 1982, and was succeeded by Yuri V. Andropov (who was elected secretary general of the Communist party on November 12 and head of state seven months later). In some respects, however, the question of succession does not yet appear to have been definitively settled. Nor has the Soviet economy, which badly needs streamlining, responded as yet to impulses for sustained improvement.

Changes in leadership in the Federal Republic of Germany and in the Soviet Union to this date have not led to significant shifts in their respective foreign policy priorities. East-West relations and relations within the Western alliance, however, have grown more tense as the time for deployment of middle-range nuclear systems has approached. Since there is but faint hope that the United States and the Soviet Union will compose their differences in the Geneva intermediate-range nuclear force (INF) talks, deployment should commence, as foreseen, before the end of 1983. It will not be easy to carry out--especially in the Federal Republic of Germany--in the face of massive and continuing opposition from the peace movement, the Greens, and the Social Democratic party. But barring totally unforeseeable circumstances, the West German government should be able to honor its commitment to the stationing of American missiles.

The shooting down of a Korean airliner by Soviet interceptor aircraft on September 1, 1983, is too recent an event to analyze adequately. This incident is bound to aggravate relations between the superpowers and thus have an adverse effect on alliance relations as well, but I doubt the effects will be long lasting. The consequences of U.S. missile deployment will, in any event, be serious. The Soviet Union will undoubtedly implement countermeasures with which it has threatened the West. The two powers may not abandon arms control and reduction talks altogether, but a temporary interruption of such talks is likely.

The political climate in post-deployment Europe will definitely be chilly, and the prospect for improvement in U.S.-Soviet relations will be dimmer still than a year ago. In Western Europe, polarization between political forces who support and oppose American nuclear systems may be expected. The terms and conditions for developing harmonious relations between America and its allies will be further strained. The tasks of devising viable policies for interacting with the East will also become more onerous but not fundamentally different from what they were in the past.

NATO: Trends and Alternatives
July 1982

GENERAL CONSIDERATIONS

The North Atlantic Treaty Organization (NATO) is currently in the throes of a profound crisis, which veteran observers tend to identify as more threatening to its very survival than any of the numerous instances of serious dissension among member states in the past. Yet the alliance does not appear to be in danger of dissolution. Public opinion in Europe does not seem to deviate appreciably over the question of remaining within the alliance. Throughout the years, 70 percent or more of the citizens of various countries who have been asked whether they favor their respective country's continued adherence to NATO answered in the affirmative. Despite unprecedented public agitation concerning the stationing of middle-range nuclear missiles on the European continent in recent years, contemporary public opinion surveys reveal sustained, solid support for continuing membership in the alliance. The question, then, is not whether the voting constituency of any country wishes to mandate its government to withdraw from the alliance, but in what form the alliance is most likely to survive? And how viable is it likely to be?

As an alliance of democratic states, NATO must always be sensitive to the political considerations that motivate the actions of its members. The viability of NATO as an instrument of common defense against external aggression is a concomitant of the political will of those who have joined voluntarily to provide for their collective security. Member governments are trustees of their respective constituencies, and while they can and do exercise the prerogatives of leadership, their effectiveness--not to say their tenure in office--is a function of their ability to generate public support for their policies. Political acceptability has always been the touchstone of successful defense policy in democratic systems. This is perhaps more evident at present than it has been in bygone years. Defense issues now attract greater public attention than ever and are more closely, although not necessarily more dispassionately, scrutinized and debated by an aroused citizenry. The public is in part

more alert to the implications of the military policies
to which its government is committed, and it is in part
more bewildered by uncertainties concerning the future.
The current popular debate, carried on in somewhat
shrill tones and in a crisis atmosphere, gained momentum under the impact of precipitous international developments that began to unfold at the end of 1979.
These developments shattered a climate of optimistic
expectations that had spread over Western Europe in the
1970s. What many Europeans had come to regard as a
firmly entrenched condition of stability in East-West
relations on the continent proved ephemeral after all.
Gradual progress toward an improvement of political,
economic, and human contacts (on a multilateral basis,
in a setting of balanced military power between the
superpowers) ground to a halt. The debate has not been
confined to national boundaries. It has transcended
these and has acquired the character of a predominantly
transatlantic dispute between the United States and its
NATO allies. That, perhaps, is putting it a little too
simply, for it implies the existence of something akin
to a monolithic West European set of views and attitudes, which is not quite the case. Divisions of
opinion exist within all countries and among European
countries, in addition to the transatlantic chasm which
troubles the alliance.
There is no single root cause of the travail in
which the alliance currently labors. Nevertheless, it
is clear that the demonstrated aggressive propensities
of the Soviet Union blatantly expressed in Afghanistan
rank highest on the list of contributing factors, the
more so as Soviet aggression in Afghanistan dramati-
cally underscored the global military might of the USSR
and brought into sharp focus Soviet military superiority in Europe as well.
As a direct result of Soviet aggression in Afghanistan, the processes of interaction between the
United States and the USSR took on the air of a punitive crusade conducted by Washington against Moscow.
In Europe, where it was widely felt that the Soviet
Union had violated the rules of the game as understood
and interpreted by the West, there was only moderate
inclination (if any) to join in a punitive crusade.
For the notion of crime and punishment--particularly as
applied to a superpower--is not consistent with European perceptions of what guiding concepts should be
in international affairs. Serious policy disagreements
surfaced between America and its West European allies.
Disputes and tensions which had arisen in the
course of the 1970s, largely as a consequence of substantially different experiences which the United
States and Western European countries (particularly the
Federal Republic of Germany) had accumulated in their

respective relations with the Soviet Union in the framework of detente, now became exacerbated. Both sides, the United States on the one hand and the West European countries on the other hand, articulated their grievances (some of which were of long standing) and tended to consider the other side's policies as ill conceived. Europeans thought that the United States was overreacting to the Soviet's admittedly bad behavior and was confining its policy options vis-a-vis the Soviet Union too narrowly to the military field. The United States, in turn, expressed increasing dismay at the seeming indifference of Europeans in the face of Soviet aggression; at their misguided insistence on seeking to preserve the gains they thought they had made in political, economic, and human relations with the Soviet Union; and at their commensurately downgrading the seriousness of the Soviet military menace that was palpably staring in their face. In short, a climate of suspicion overtook the alliance in which mutual recriminations escalated. Under the circumstances, European public opinion became very perturbed and susceptible to skillful manipulation by Soviet and communist propaganda.

Through a curious but not entirely incomprehensible distortion, many Europeans came to hold the United States responsible for the deterioration of East-West relations. The truculence of the American government, which, if anything, grew more vehement under the administration of President Reagan, served as a ready pretext for those who wished to shunt the blame for the U.S.-Soviet standoff to Washington rather than to Moscow. The fate suffered by the LRTNF modernization decision adopted by the foreign and defense ministers of the member states of NATO on December 12, 1979 (a delay of nearly two years before the start of INF talks between the United States and the USSR), turned out to be the prime mover of the spread of anti-American sentiments in Europe. It provided a rallying point for various peace groups that proliferated in this period and attracted massive popular support.

EUROPEAN PEACE MOVEMENTS

It would be farfetched to say that European peace movements are the creations of the past few years. They were much in evidence in the late 1950s when nuclear testing was the chief target of their invocations and have not disappeared since, although they tended to fade into the landscape and were quiescent during most of the period of detente in Europe (that is, practically throughout the 1970s). They were galvanized into action in 1977-78 by the campaign against the enhanced radiation weapon (ERW), which in popular parlance was known as the "neutron bomb." The characteristics of

Neutron bomb puts European peace movement in the forefront.

this weapon, highly touted by its inventors, gave rise to widespread outrage. A weapon that killed people but did not damage property, including instruments of war (such as tanks), was certain to cause a feeling of revulsion among many. Seen in hindsight, the anti-neutron bomb campaign (in which the Soviet Union and foreign Communist parties were deeply involved) was but a dress rehearsal for the anti-nuclear campaign of the 1980s.

This is not the proper place to attempt a thoroughgoing dissection of the anatomy and analysis of the physiology of peace movements in Europe (or in the United States, where the movement has become vocal), if a reliable account of the anatomy and physiology of such heterogeneous movements were as yet even possible. There are some common denominators among them, most significantly, perhaps, an inclination of their adherents toward pacifism or "unilateralism" in questions of disarmament. Further, there is an unquestionable moral, ethical, and religious constituent element that is part of all peace movements, albeit in varying proportions. And there are other, more highly politicized, ideologically motivated, or otherwise alienated advocacy groups and individuals who are attracted to the peace movement as an outlet through which they can express themselves. Hans Rühle, director of the Social Science Research Institute of the Konrad Adenauer Foundation in St. Augustin (near Bonn), observed that the "issue has become a magnet for the convergence of several forces--radical socialist, pacifist, environmentalist, neutralist, and even religious."[1]

Manfred Wörner, a Christian Democratic deputy in the West German Bundestag, characterized the peace movement of his country as a "variegated phenomenon" and distinguished among no less than five basic categories of pacifist currents in the German peace movement:

1. Pacifism of faith *religious*
2. Pacifism of fear *environmentalist*
3. Pacifism of welfare *radical socialists*
4. Pacifism of expedience, whose representatives take their orders straight from Moscow
5. Reunification pacifism, which might also be called a "nationalist-neutralist" pacifism[2]

In no two countries has the genesis and development of the peace movement been exactly alike. In Holland, for example, the Dutch Reformed Church (the country's leading religious denomination) espoused an anti-nuclear stance as early as 1962, and the current spearhead of the anti-nuclear movement is the Interkerkelijk Vredesberaad or IKV (Interchurch Council on

[handwritten margin note, left side, vertical]: Convergence of people operating under various motivations in the peace movement

[handwritten note, bottom]: Holland's predominant church is at the head of that country's peace movement.

Matters of Peace and War). The IKV was formed in 1967 on the initiative of a working group from the Dutch Reformed Church and the Roman Catholic Pax Christi group.[3]

In the Federal Republic of Germany, according to Manfred Wörner, the real genesis of the peace movement "goes back to the Soviet invasion of Afghanistan in late 1979--and to the subsequent 'war-is-in-sight' theme adopted by the governing SPD [Social Democratic party] in the electoral campaigns of 1980--a theme that reached a climax in Chancellor Schmidt's articulated efforts to liken the situation of 1980 to that of 1914, on the eve of World War I."[4]

In some European countries, particularly those with a strong Protestant tradition, the church does seem integrally involved in the anti-nuclear movement. (Incidentally, this is also true in the German Democratic Republic where the peace movement is, of course, not permitted to operate overtly.) In predominantly Catholic countries in Europe (such as Italy or France) the church is less involved, and the peace movement also appears to have less vigor than elsewhere. But in the United States, which is also a predominantly Protestant country, Catholic prelates have been in the forefront of the movement advocating a freeze on all nuclear weapons development.

Caution is also required in attempting broad generalizations about the numerical strength of national peace movements, the social and vocational status, and the age and sex composition of their adherents. Trade unions are strongly peace-oriented in some countries, but not in others. Women and men are, perhaps, involved in equal numbers. On the whole, young people are more apt to participate actively in peace demonstrations, but older people support the aims of the peace movement in proportions that are not significantly different from those of younger age groups. Nor is it possible to draw sharp lines of demarcation in the peace movement in terms of the traditional left-right political spectrum. To be sure, radical splinter groups are heavily represented in the peace movement, and within "leftist" parties--such as the British Labor party or the West German Social Democratic party--there is widespread anti-nuclear sentiment. But the West German Social Democratic party in its majority has to date given formal support to Chancellor Schmidt's unequivocal public stance in favor of LRTNF modernization.[5] In Italy, but particularly in France, the Socialist parties do not have an anti-nuclear orientation. In Holland, however, the Labor party is hostile to the stationing of both middle- and short-range nuclear weapons in its country, and in Scandinavia, Socialists generally oppose deployment. Anti-nuclear factions may also be found in conservative parties.

In predominately Protestant Europe the churches are at the front of the movement; but in the U.S., it is the Catholic Church.

SOVIET EFFORTS TO INFLUENCE EUROPEAN PEACE MOVEMENTS

Given the Kremlin's propensity to seek advantage by exploiting political opportunities as these present themselves, it would be surprising indeed if the Soviet Union did not exert itself to the utmost to impinge on and influence peace movements in Western Europe, the United States, and everywhere else in the world.

The leading role played by the Soviet Union in launching the anti-neutron bomb campaign is relatively easy to document. TASS (the Soviet news agency which often serves as a government mouthpiece when other institutions seem less suitable to act in this capacity) called for the initiation of an anti-neutron bomb campaign on July 30, 1977. Dutifully following suit, the World Peace Council (a communist front organization which Stalin created in 1949 and to which he attributed special significance as an auxiliary tool of Soviet foreign policy) proclaimed an action week of anti-neutron bomb agitation for August 6-13. On August 8, twenty-eight European Communist parties issued a common appeal to all Socialists, Social Democrats, and Christians to join in the struggle against the neutron bomb. Individual Communist parties--for example, the Dutch, which until then had been seriously estranged from the Soviet Union--followed up with national appeals in their respective countries.[6]

There is overwhelming evidence that the Soviet Union and Communist parties in its tow are heavily involved in the anti-nuclear peace campaigns of the 1980s, but documentation of the degree and manner of their involvement is, for the time being, fragmentary rather than comprehensive.

The Soviet Union pursues the unmistakable objective of whipping up anti-nuclear sentiment, to such a degree as to cause it to prevail on European governments to reconsider the decision they adopted in December 1979 and to cancel the deployment of middle-range nuclear missiles on the territory of their countries.

In pursuit of this objective, the Soviet Union resorts to a wide variety of tactics:

1. Periodic proclamations by President Brezhnev couched in "reasonable" terms, expressing solicitude for the concern people have for the preservation of peace and suggesting almost unconditional readiness on the part of the Soviet Union to assist in removing the threat of war that blights people's lives.[7]

2. Propaganda campaigns through the conventional channels of Soviet media which elaborate on and reinforce President Brezhnev's tantalizing and suggestive messages. These campaigns contrast the Soviet Union's "sincere" desire for peace with the manifest belligerence of the United States, compare

the policies of the superpowers in a light unfavorable to the United States, and exhort people of good
will to join forces against the unleashing of a new
war.
3. Publication of special and easily obtainable pam-
phlets that treat the danger of war in Europe com-
prehensively, with apparent objectivity and excep-
tional sophistication.[8]
4. Utilization of high-level spokesmen (with a thorough
knowledge of Western countries and their languages)
possessing considerable professional skill in dealing with European publics, to lend credibility to
President Brezhnev's messages. These spokesmen
approach their tasks with unprecedented openness;
they are available to Western journalists and
readily grant interviews for publication in Western
newspapers or airing on Western radio and television
programs.[9]
5. Sponsorship of a wide variety of international meetings bearing on the simple theme of preserving the
peace and thereby saving mankind from a nuclear
holocaust.
6. Participation in international forums concerned with
the preservation of peace, organized by groups that
are not communist fronts.
7. Assistance to Communist parties overtly at open and
publicized party gatherings or covertly through
concealed agents, in the planning and execution of
anti-nuclear campaigns and demonstrations.
8. Allocation of financial resources through covert
agents for the printing of anti-nuclear literature,
the placement of advertisements, and so forth.

Supervision and implementation of the aforemen-
tioned activities is concentrated in the Secretariat of
the Communist party of the Soviet Union and in special
institutions established by the party for the stated
purpose.
Within the party's Secretariat, the International
Department is chiefly responsible for contacts with
foreign Communist parties and communist front organizations. To raise the level of effectiveness in getting
information to foreign audiences, a new International
Information Department was recently created in the
party's Secretariat. It is headed by Leonid M.
Zamyatin, the former director general of TASS who has
also served as a member of the Soviet diplomatic service in the Federal Republic of Germany.
Broader contacts with peace groups and the preparation of special literature is in the purview of the
Soviet Committee for European Security and Cooperation,
which has available to it the services of a scientific
council for the study of problems related to peace,
arms reduction, and control.

The importance which is attached to participation in international peace forums is reflected by the high caliber of the delegates who represent the Soviet Union there. For example, an international conference against nuclear weapons was recently held in Japan, at which such topical issues as problems of curbing the threat of nuclear war, ending the arms race, and consolidating international security were discussed. The chief Soviet delegate to the conference was Yevgeniy M. Tyazhelnikov, head of the party's Propaganda Department, and he was accompanied by Ivan I. Kovalenko, one of the deputy heads of the party's International Department. Also, Georgi A. Arbatov, head of the Institute of U.S. and Canadian Studies of the Soviet Academy of Sciences and a full member of the party's Central Committee, was the Soviet member of the Independent Commission of Disarmament and Security, better known as the Palme Commission (after its chairman, Swedish political leader Olaf Palme).

While the Soviet Union does not limit its efforts to any one country or any given group, it does seem to concentrate heavily on the Federal Republic of Germany, which occupies a pivotal place in NATO. Evidence to this effect can be found, among other things, in the extraordinary attention given to and close guidance provided for the minuscule DKP, the German Communist party, which in its own right is an insignificant political and social force in the Federal Republic of Germany. For example, the DKP Congress held in Hannover in April 1981 was attended by no lesser personalities than Boris N. Ponomarev and Vadim V. Zagladin. Ponomarev held responsible positions in the Secretariat of the Comintern in the 1930s and was a close collaborator of Stalin's in international Communist affairs. He is now an alternate member of the Politburo as well as a secretary of the Communist party and head of its International Department. Zagladin is Ponomarev's deputy and likely successor. Congresses of small and insignificant parties are usually attended by lower ranking party officials, and they do not receive effusive and lengthy treatment as _Pravda_ accorded to the gathering of the DKP.

Furthermore, there can be no doubt that the DKP and its supporters initiated and inspired the so-called Krefelder Appell (Krefeld Appeal), adopted at a forum on November 15, 1980, in the town of Krefeld. The Krefeld Appeal openly calls on the West German government to renounce its concurrence in "the deployment of Pershing II and cruise missiles in Central Europe." In its conceptions and implementation, it is closely patterned after communist-sponsored campaigns against imperialism and fascism in the 1930s. To date, it is reported that over a million signatures have been collected for the appeal.[10]

The effectiveness of the Soviet Union's exertions
cannot be reliably evaluated. The peace movement is
too diffuse and too large to be dominated by Communists. Yet the thrust of anti-nuclear agitation--
especially in its anti-American aspects--does coincide
with Soviet interests. This is unfortunate, for it
helps to confuse rather than to clarify issues and
thereby compounds the problems of the Western alliance.
The fact that there are signs of dissension between
Communists and non-Communists in the peace movement is
small solace, though such dissension may in the long
run not be unimportant. Anti-nuclear agitation which
tended to be aimed exclusively at the United States has
been recently more evenhandedly directed against both
superpowers. The Soviet government has grudgingly had
to make concessions to peace advocates who have sought
entry into the Soviet Union to demonstrate there, in
far smaller numbers than in Western capitals, but visible to the Soviet population just the same. Inclined
to prohibit such demonstrations, Soviet authorities
have had to countenance them (although under tightly
controlled conditions and with severe constraints on
the demonstrators) for fear of losing credibility and
undermining their own efforts in the West.

Whatever involvement the peace movement may have
with the Soviet Union and Communists subservient to it,
the very existence of the movement and the dynamism it
has displayed reflect a sudden escalation of public
consciousness brought about by the inexorable spread of
nuclear weapons.

POLITICAL IMPERATIVES IN INTRA-ALLIANCE RELATIONS

The recent rise in public consciousness may not
represent a "fundamental change" as Erhard Eppler, an
ardent left-wing West German Social Democratic champion
of the peace movement, contends.[11] It is, however,
substantial and is not likely to subside soon. Hence-
forth, the political acceptability of military solutions affecting the vital security interests of the
alliance will have to be given far greater consideration. The terms and conditions of political accepta-
bility--the criteria by which proposed solutions will
be judged--have to be explicitly understood, particularly by American leaders, if the alliance is to be
saved from inflicting wounds on itself. The task of
bringing the military and political dimensions of
NATO's security policies into proper harmony is formidable at best. It is complicated by the constantly
growing complexities of deterrence logic, which makes
it ever more difficult to explain the perplexity that
lies at the heart of military deterrence.[12]

In these circumstances, the gap between public
perceptions and the reality of military needs tends to

widen, and political problems arise. These problems are not limited to the peace movement. They engulf the entire population, including many (if not all) of their leaders. Shrill as the peace movement is, it does not speak for the whole nation in any country, although it does play a significant role as a catalyst. In the Federal Republic of Germany, for example, the contentious LRTNF decision is the major source of anti-nuclear agitation. It was approved in a recent public opinion poll by 36 percent of those interviewed, while 21 percent opposed it, 12 percent were indifferent, and 30 percent claimed to have no opinion. How is one to interpret these results? Is a 36 percent approval rate abysmally low? Is it a signal for retreat? Would the LRTNF decision be upheld if it were submitted to a nationwide referendum? Or is the fact that those who approve have a better than three-to-two majority over those who disapprove to be interpreted in a more positive light?[13]

Most likely, the answers to this simple question taken in isolation--which is always somewhat risky for interpretive purposes--show above all how divided and confused the German population is (30 percent claim to have no opinion!) on the issue of LRTNF modernization. An interesting aspect of the answers is that they show remarkably small differences in preference among members of the established political parties. Thus, the approval rate among members of the CDU is 38 percent; SPD, 37 percent; FDP (the liberal Free Democratic party), 35 percent. The disapproval rate is CDU, 18 percent; SPD, 22 percent; FDP, 23 percent. Significantly different answers are given only by those who adhere to the new political grouping--the Greens--among whom 17 percent approve, 60 percent disapprove, 3 percent are indifferent, and 20 percent have no opinion. The Greens in combination with the so-called Alternatives (a left radical combination) have polled 6-8 percent of the vote in recent state elections in Berlin (1981), Lower Saxony (March 1982), and Hamburg (June 1982), and have qualified for representation in the legislative assemblies of these states.

How can the issues pertaining to the defense requirements of the alliance be put more clearly and credibly, so that the public will both understand them better and accept them as justified in the context of its perceptions of national priorities? These priorities surely include economic stability and social welfare, perhaps not at the risk of jeopardizing national security, but not in a subordinate relationship to military expenditures.

The responsibility for providing convincing answers falls mainly on the United States, by far the strongest military power in the alliance, the titular and real leader of NATO. Contrary to what one might be inclined to think in America, the burdens of leadership do not entitle the United States to commensurate prerogatives of leadership. The United States cannot dictate to its allies and should not try to browbeat them. It must win their consent for common policies and persuade them in consultation.

America's problems are compounded by many factors; among them are some that are not susceptible to change, such as the geo-strategic structure of the alliance. The perspective in which the Soviet threat is seen is different from the two shores of the Atlantic. Europeans tend to have horizons limited to their region. Americans, in turn, are more apt to see the Soviet Union in a global setting and to link Soviet behavior in various parts of the world. With a growing preoccupation over the global responsibilities of the United States to counter that threat, misunderstandings can readily develop between Washington and West European capitals. Tempers flare, mutual accusations--which the alliance can ill afford--abound.[14]

Substantial differences of opinion between the United States and its West European allies manifest themselves less in the assessment of the military power which the Soviet Union has steadily built up than in the expectation of how likely the Soviet Union is to use its military power in Europe.[15]

Perhaps more significantly still, there is a sharp divergence of judgments about what Western policies toward the Soviet Union should be and how they should be applied.

FORTRESS AMERICA AND NEUTRALISM IN EUROPE

Among divisive trends within the alliance, neutralism, which might develop in certain European states, and isolationism (or a resurgence of the concept of "fortress America"), which might spread in the United States, would be the most damaging. In a curious way, neutralist tendencies in Europe and isolationist proclivities in America feed on each other. Growing perceptions of neutralist trends in Europe give added impetus to an isolationist mood in the United States, which finds expression in the advocacy of U.S. withdrawal from Europe and abandonment of Europeans to a fate which they brought upon themselves and well deserve. In turn, such signs of isolationism as European countries attribute to the United States induce and strengthen existing inclinations toward neutralism, particularly in countries that do not possess any independent nuclear means to deter aggression or defend against it. These countries are--to a heightened degree, if not totally--dependent upon the American

Neutralist trends in Europe feed American isolationism and vice-versa.

nuclear shield. The Federal Republic of Germany is a case in point, although it is not alone among non-nuclear states in Europe.

Although neutralism in Europe and isolationism in the United States nurture and mutually reinforce each other, other causes may also induce the rise of these tendencies. In Europe neutralism is enhanced as a means (perhaps the only means) of escaping involvement in war by widespread feelings that the United States is chiefly responsible for an exacerbation of international tensions. Belligerent American attitudes toward the Soviet Union are seen as increasing the danger of war in Europe. Conversely, in the United States isolationism does reflect a sense that Europeans are insufficiently alert to the military danger that confronts them on the part of Soviet and Warsaw Pact forces and that they stubbornly refuse to contribute adequately to their own defense.

This sentiment is forcefully reflected in a study issued under the auspices of the Institute of Foreign Policy Analysis, which among other things asserts that "key European allies—notably Germany and the Low Countries, where most U.S. forces in Europe are stationed—are failing to do their part for common defense." The authors of the study recommend "that the time has come for the United States to begin withdrawing most of its ground forces from Europe." One of the authors, retired Admiral Robert J. Hanks (in an apparent justification of this recommendation) seems to take for granted the conquest of Western Europe by the Soviet Union as a consequence of U.S. troop withdrawal from the continent. In his view, this would be a severe blow to the United States, but it would most assuredly be fatal to Western Europe.[16]

Growing impatience on the part of Americans with their European allies is aggravated by two additional conditions: the global challenge of Soviet military power, which is unprecedented and confronts the United States with an entirely new set of military problems; and the concomitant, deeply felt fiscal pinch on resources that are available to build up the military forces of the United States, as needed.

Scarcity of fiscal resources is a common denominator among all NATO allies. The failure of Europeans to spend more on their defense is conditioned to some extent by fear that greater military budgets (assuming that they are justified by legitimate needs to fend off the Soviet military threat) would strain the resources at their disposal. Greater outlays for the military could be achieved only at the expense of social supports which they—in contrast to the United States—consider vital for the preservation of internal political stability. Massive social instability could entail far-reaching consequences in Europe, and the concern

West European governments have about the potential
destabilizing influence of social unrest in their countries, although perhaps exaggerated, is rooted in his-
torical experience.

To what extent isolationism will spread in the
United States and will dominate American commitments to
Europe in the foreseeable future remains to be seen.
It can hardly be doubted that a substantial revision of
the magnitude and terms of the U.S. contribution to the
defense of Western Europe would have a significant
impact on NATO. The alliance would probably dis-
integrate.

It is also impossible to anticipate with any degree of accuracy to what extent neutralism will spread
among European populations. At the moment, there is no
indication that neutralism is advocated anywhere by
significant and influential groups or political parties. "Hollanditis" is a term of derision that implies
an advanced state of torpor in regard to defense mea-
sures--if not a penchant for unilateral disarmament--
typical of its country of origin, Holland, but also
observable elsewhere.[17] The term distorts the existing reality of things, not just in the Netherlands but
also in neighboring and Scandinavian countries.

The Dutch resent the term as a misleading and
insulting description of a misunderstood situation.
The picture evoked by Hollanditis is that of a disease
that can be recognized by symptoms such as an un-
willingness to spend enough money on defense, a fear of
taking necessary decisions in the field of nuclear
armaments, and a general tendency toward neutralism and
pacifism. It is damaging to Holland and odious to the
Dutch, because it belittles a genuine concern about the
destructive potential of nuclear weapons and the
frightening perspective of nuclear war. It exposes to
ridicule those who seek to take these concerns into
account in developing national security policies that
would at once be adequate to the task of staving off an
aggressor and of reassuring the population that peace
will not wantonly be sacrificed for the sake of military adventurism.

In the Federal Republic of Germany, neutralist
sentiment can draw on certain historic precedents with
a strong nationalistic tinge. Germans traditionally
did not feel that they were part of the "West" nor, of
course, did they identify with the"East." They stood
in between and exalted the notion of "Mitteleuropa"
(Central Europe), where they held sway. Yet the integration of the Federal Republic of Germany into the
Western alliance system following World War II is more
than a passing, superficial phenomenon. Neutralism may
have some appeal to various groups of frustrated individuals who are alienated from the existing political
order and who do not support their country's alignment.

It is not likely, however, to capture the imagination
of the vast majority of the population, which readily
recognizes the threat to national sovereignty that
would ensue if they detached themselves from the Western alliance system and attempted to "go it alone."
    Even if European politicians occasionally threaten
their American counterparts with the prospect of irresistible unilateralism in Europe, rampant neutralism
on the continent does not menace the stability of the
alliance. In the worst case, if one or two smaller
countries were to detach themselves from NATO (an extreme and hardly foreseeable eventuality) or simply
cease to function as effective members of the alliance
without formally withdrawing from it, the damage to the
structure of the alliance would be minor compared to
that inflicted by an estrangement of the United States
from its West European allies.

NEW BILATERAL AND MULTILATERAL AGREEMENTS?

    Attempts to restructure the alliance through new
bilateral or multilateral agreements may surface peri-
odically and find expression in various proposals that
would seek to draw the European members into some sort
of closer partnership, with the aim of balancing the
influence--if not the power--of the United States. The
success of such schemes, however, is bound to be limited, due to lack of sufficient support among the
larger countries. This does not rule out the endeavor
to create something akin to a pressure group of smaller
states within NATO, speaking with a single voice or, at
any rate, acting with conscious coordination of their
policies in order to carry more weight in alliance deliberations. Such an arrangement would not have a major impact on the basic structure of the alliance, and
the policies advocated by a consortium of smaller countries would not necessarily be at odds with those of
the alliance as a whole.
    Bilateral military cooperation between France and
the Federal Republic of Germany emerges from time to
time as a possible solution to the problems of both
countries, in regard to their defense posture and obligations. France, however, is not likely to sacrifice
the relative freedom of action it enjoys under current
circumstances nor to share control of its nuclear arsenal with another country, least of all with the Federal Republic of Germany. The Federal Republic, in
turn, would gain little from a closer military alliance
with France at the expense of the protection which it
now derives from its membership in NATO.
    Multilateral agreements that would transcend the
realm of Western Europe and would involve other countries (for example, in the framework of the Helsinki
agreement), though not entirely unattractive, could not

serve as a substitute for NATO. Progress toward multilateral cooperation in a European framework might reduce tensions between competing power blocs in Europe
and as such would be generally welcome. But such progress, if any, would not create preconditions for dis-
solving the existing European alliance systems.

ARMS CONTROL AND DISARMAMENT NEGOTIATIONS

Multilateral talks about arms control and disarmament in Europe have so far not been held, but they
have been gaining favor in an increasing number of
countries. A Europe-wide disarmament conference is on
the agenda in Madrid, where the thirty-five signatory
powers of the Helsinki agreement have been wrangling--
mostly over human rights--since 1980. Should this
(second) follow-up meeting to the Conference on Security and Cooperation in Europe (CSCE) lead to a successful conclusion, the way to a Conference on Disarmament in Europe (CDE) would be cleared. Participation of a large number of countries that are not members of either NATO or of the Warsaw Pact might have
potential advantages over bilateral (superpower) or
modified multilateral discussions that have a bloc-to-
bloc character. But the range of issues that could be
discussed in a broader forum probably would be more
limited.[18]

The Mutual and Balanced Force Reduction Talks in
Vienna (MBFR), in which eighteen NATO and Warsaw Pact
countries are participating, are modified multilateral
negotiations with a bloc-to-bloc character. (MBFR is
extensively discussed in chapter two.) Although visible results in the form of an agreement are lacking
after nine years of uninterrupted negotiation, the
Vienna talks have helped to clarify significant problems and have brought about a reconciliation of views
on major issues. An agreement in Vienna would have
limited effect. Among other things, it would not alleviate military problems that affect the Northern and
Southern flanks of NATO (particularly Norway and Turkey). But a reduction of troops on the central front,
where NATO and the Warsaw Pact have assembled and have
kept in place a massive concentration of military
forces, might have a salutary impact on the political
climate in Europe and a beneficial influence on relations among members of the Western alliance.

Bilateral arms control negotiations between the
United States and the Soviet Union have not yielded
positive results that would have enhanced the security
of NATO. The failure of arms control to help produce a
more secure military environment has actually become a
source of tension and disagreement, blighting alliance
relations. Europeans have been reluctant to acquiesce
in the abandonment of arms control as an instrument of

Western policy, despite disappointing experiences with
this type of "confidence building" between NATO and the
Warsaw Pact. Americans have developed serious doubts
about arms control as a suitable means for reaching
accord with the Soviet Union.

With scaled-down expectations of what could be accomplished through arms control negotiations, Europeans
may be able to have a greater forbearance for the
frustration of the United States, which has borne the
burden of dealing with the Soviet Union. The United
States, for its part, may be able to display greater
tolerance for European attitudes that demonstrate a
strong attachment to the continuation of arms control
efforts. It is important for the United States to pre-
serve--or regain, as the case may be--credibility in
the eyes of those Europeans who have become skeptical
about America's good faith in pursuing arms control
objectives.

The absence of tangible results over a long period
may still give rise to political agitation in various
European countries. This could cause friction in the
alliance, even if delay were due to Soviet rather than
American obstreperousness. Attentive European publics
may be expected to monitor arms control negotiations
much more closely than in the past, and it would be
prudent to anticipate that public perceptions of the
arms control process will significantly bear on domestic politics, affecting the behavior of political parties and guiding the actions of elected governments.
It would serve the best interests of the United States
and its European allies if they managed to prevent
bilateral U.S.-Soviet negotiations about strategic and
intermediate-range nuclear forces from exerting persistent and major disruptive influence on the alliance.

DECLINE OF NATO ALLIANCE?   CONTINUATION OF STATUS QUO?

As matters now stand, it does not seem likely that
the alliance will soon--and without considerable exer-
tion--overcome the baneful effects of its nuclear dilemma. Disagreements about the ends that should be
sought and the means best suited to achieve these ends
constitute a source of irritation that could lead to a
decline of the alliance. It is not certain that the
overriding common interests and purposes of the member
states, which have sustained the alliance over a remarkably long period, will continue to provide an adequate framework for the preservation of the status quo.

Not that the fundamental premises that underlay
the creation of NATO in the late 1940s have lost their
validity. Now, as then, the member states of the
alliance share a dedication to political democracy and
human rights in the context of a market economy. It is
this dedication that primarily distinguishes them from

the Soviet Communist system and the Communist systems
of the East European member states of the Warsaw Pact.

The terms and conditions of struggle between the
two competing power blocs in Europe--NATO and the Warsaw Pact--have not changed in their essence. The military potential of the Soviet Union, considered to be
formidable in the immediate aftermath of World War II,
has grown more formidable still, as a result of a relentless armament effort. An abundance of nuclear weapons on both sides introduces a menacing dimension
into the military equation, which was not present in
earlier times when the United States had overwhelming
nuclear superiority.

The main mission of NATO is to safeguard the
Western alliance against an external military threat
and to this end provide for an adequate deterrent and
defense capability. The question is how one defines
adequacy, and that is not a trivial matter on which
automatic consensus is easy to obtain. Both military
posture and military strategy are subject to varying
interpretations that need to be reconciled.

A second set of considerations, introduced in 1967
by the famed Harmel Report (so named after the Belgian
foreign minister who chaired the NATO commission that
submitted the report), must also be kept in mind. The
thrust of the Harmel Report was that in addition to its
military mission, NATO had a political mission in maintaining peace. The peace-keeping functions of NATO are
perforce less sharply defined than its military mission
and more difficult to implement, as NATO lacks the
institutional infrastructure and procedural experience
to deal with the political aspects of peace keeping on
an ongoing basis. The fact that NATO is really not a
supranational alliance whose sovereignty supersedes
that of its individual members tends to hamper the
development of unified policies uniformly implemented
by the member states. The whole (that is, the alliance) is smaller than the sum of its parts. While it
would be undesirable to subordinate the member states
to a single command structure (and futile to attempt to
do so), it would be useful to develop permanent consul-
tative mechanisms for coordinating political and economic strategies. This would help to overcome difficulties which the alliance has been chronically experiencing.

In any event, a protracted confrontation between
opposing power blocs, armed to the teeth with an array
of the most destructive weapons yet produced by the
ingenuity of human beings, is not an ideal condition
for nurturing the very principles and values which the
Western democracies hope to protect against an outside
enemy. In fact, it is not an acceptable condition of
existence for the European democracies, who live in
close physical proximity to the Soviet Union and its

East European allies. The democracies are impelled to
seek a tolerable modus vivendi with the adversary by
finding viable means of interaction and political accommodation. Given the nature of the adversary, such
accommodation may be attainable only at the price of
appeasement. This is the dilemma of the Western alliance, which it must somehow resolve.

Western Europe between the Superpowers
September 1982

I

In reality, there is no such political, economic,
social, or cultural entity as Western Europe, let alone
Europe. Yet all European countries (West and East) do
share some common features. This is not to say that
the two alliance systems can be reduced to a common
denominator. Far from it. But in their own right,
both systems are experiencing very similar problems.
All countries--not just members of the adversary alliances but nonaligned (like Yugoslavia) and neutrals
(like Austria and Sweden)--are in the throes of major
economic difficulties. These threaten the internal
stability of individual countries and the stability of
the respective alliances. By the same token, the equi-
librium which has existed on the continent in one
form or another ever since the unconditional surrender of Hitler's Third Reich in 1945 is perhaps in
greater jeopardy than at any time since the end of
World War II.
In addition to their economic woes, both alliances
are experiencing a crisis of confidence between the
leading power and the lesser members of the alliance,
although the structures of these alliances are very
different as are the processes by which their members
interact. These differences must not be lost from
sight in attempting to analyze the manner in which the
internal problems of the respective alliances may be
solved.
It may be argued, for example, that at least the
problems facing the two alliances in the military realm
can hardly be compared. While in the West questions
pertaining to the degree of military effort that is
required to safeguard the security of the alliance
constitute a significant source of debate (not to say
of dissension), in the East there is scant evidence
that this subject is a contentious one. This, however,
does not imply the existence of a unanimous opinion
about military questions, and the viability of the

Warsaw Pact as an instrument for purposes of all types of military undertakings should not be taken for granted. The only constant--which has shown no signs of change--is an unrelenting increase in the overall military capability of the Soviet Union. Certainly this is a factor that must be treated with utmost seriousness. In the final analysis, it may be the decisive element in determining the fate of all Europe. But this is not inevitably and not fatalistically so, at least not within the next decade.

My contention would be that for the time being neither side possesses decisive advantages over the other, that one is not in upswing while the other is in decline. In many respects they are both in decline. Both need to turn inward to attend to pressing internal problems. This imparts a certain symmetry to the totality of the East-West relationship in Europe. The advantages of one side (military on the part of the East) are offset by advantages on the other side (economic on the part of the West). The East-West struggle in Europe remains open-ended.

II

Political conditions in Western Europe during the coming decade will be influenced most significantly by the following:

1. Socio-economic problems that are, strictly speaking, not a function of the East-West relationship
2. Political-military problems that grow primarily out of the East-West relationship

Important as the political-military problems may be, it is my guess that for the remainder of the decade West European countries will be more preoccupied with their socio-economic problems than with traditional political-military problems that grow out of the East-West relationship, including the intensity of the Soviet military threat. The issue of peace in Europe, however, will remain a topic of abiding public interest and political agitation.

Current economic indicators tell a doleful story for all West European countries, with the possible exception of Switzerland. Unemployment is high and rising, in some instances catastrophically. By the end of the decade, the number of chronically unemployed may be double what it now is. Great Britain shows the way with 3.29 million unemployed (13.4 percent of the labor force).[19] This represents an increase of nearly 20 percent over 1981. The percentage increase in the Federal Republic of Germany is more spectacular still, 41 percent over 1981, although the number of unemployed are still under 2 million (or less than 8 percent of the labor force).[20]

The Gross National Product (GNP) is virtually stagnating. Government budget deficits have reached astronomical proportions in some countries as Denmark, where the deficit equals 15 percent, and Belgium, where it is equal to 10 percent of GNP.[21] As one would expect, investments are substantially down in France, the Federal Republic of Germany, Holland, and other countries as well.

Despite occasional brave forecasts of an early upturn in the economies of the West European states, the current crisis appears to be of long duration. It is the result of a plethora of developments, some of which were and will be out of the reach of West European governments and private industrial, commercial, and financial enterprises to influence decisively. But to a large extent, the economic woes that have caught up with the Western industrial democracies of Europe (although not with them alone) stem from bad and irresponsible management, over which some measure of control could have been exercised. The fiscal practices of Western banks, in particular, leave a great deal to be desired. They are at the root of many difficulties, in a manner that is uncomfortably reminiscent of the antecedents of the great collapse of the international economy in the late 1920s and the early 1930s.

It remains to be seen if the mechanisms that allegedly have been developed since that time will function adequately to prevent an outright crash. Resources will be severely strained and unpleasant choices will have to be made. Clearly, one of the causes of problems is the expansion of social accounts that has characterized all European systems in the entire post-war period, but particularly in recent years. It is not at all certain, however, that substantial savings in social accounts can be effected. For one thing, at times of economic recession--not to say depression--the need for genuine social assistance is bound to rise. For another, given the European political systems, strong pressures from trade unions as well as Communist and Socialist parties for maintaining high levels of social assistance will persist. Governments in power, most of which have slim working majorities (that is, they are weak) will find it impractical not to at least partially accommodate these pressures.

The specter of social upheaval and political radicalization haunts European politicians. They will be strongly motivated to take preemptive measures to ward off any such eventuality and cast the social (safety) net as broadly as possible. Still, some retrenchment of swollen social accounts may be unavoidable.

Belt-tightening, however, will not be limited to the needy. The question is whether whole populations that have lived substantially beyond their means will be amenable to make the sacrifices required to sta- bilize the economies of their countries. No one can confidently predict that the point of no return (in regard to economic sacrifices) has not been passed. How will those with some affluence behave under these circumstances? Will they seek refuge elsewhere--pro- vided that an "elsewhere" can be found--and thus con- tribute to the further deterioration of their country's economy? Will potential investment capital dry up altogether, instead of priming the pump of sagging market economies? There is evidence that this may already be happening in some cases. The example of what occurred in France in the "revolutionary" year of 1968, when thousands of rich citizens fled (albeit temporarily) to Switzerland, is being repeated now under the socialist regime of President François Mitterand.[22] Other countries might soon follow suit if bad economic conditions endure, and if--as a corol- lary--money interests grow alarmed by what they per- ceive to be an increasing Soviet military threat to the West.

The tasks facing West European governments are formidable. What is involved in the current economic crisis is not a matter of simple course correction. The question is how to preserve the essentials of the market economy--incentives and rewards, motivations and goals--and reconcile these with inevitably expanding government guidance of the economy, without at the same time abridging the fundamentals of political democracy. Even if theoretical answers were readily available, and they are nowhere visible, their practical implementa- tion would be cumbersome. Some measure of social un- rest and political destabilization is certain to result from protracted economic crisis.

One potential source of trouble is the large num- ber of foreigners living in many European countries (2 million in Great Britain, 4.1 million in France, and 4.5 million in the Federal Republic of Germany). Their presence among the native population under the best of circumstances creates social tensions, although these tend to vary substantially from one country to another. With a tight labor market and diminishing resources for social assistance, such tensions will escalate. In some instances, the problems created thereby may prove insuperable.

How the fortunes of established political parties wil be affected is hazardous to predict. Communist parties in general have been in decline in Western Europe since the middle and late 1970s, when they ap- peared to be on the verge of reaping the benefits of Eurocommunism. It is possible that these parties will be revitalized, but the patent failure of the socialist economic systems in the Soviet Union and Eastern Europe does not augur well for them. Communism hardly appears to be suited to cure the economic ills of the West. The most likely victims of chronic economic troubles will be those parties that happen to be in power, regardless of their party label and ideological orientation. The most likely beneficiaries will be those parties that currently bear no government responsibility, be they socialist in some countries or conservative in others. In addition, the emergence of new groupings (not everywhere, but in some countries) which are in the offing will be hastened. These new groupings will be more in tune with the post-materialist orientation of younger people and will seek to offer genuine or trumped-up alternatives to the prevailing social and economic order. Traditional political alignments in many European countries may not be wholly uprooted, but a significant redistribution of relative influence among political parties is to be expected, as a result of socio-economic conditions and as a by-product of other problems as well.

Another outgrowth of endemic economic difficulties will be a downturn in the processes of European unification. The emergence of a truly cohesive European Economic Community (EEC), let alone a European Parliament, is not in sight. It will be postponed still further. Neither the community nor the parliament will thrive in conditions of economic adversity in which governments, perhaps contrary to their best interests, are apt to become more outspokenly nationalistic and protectionist than cooperative.

III

A fragmented Western Europe wil encounter increasing difficulties in its relations with the United States and the Soviet Union. In neither case will the West European countries be able to speak with a single, authoritative voice. This will be more detrimental to them in fending off such divisive tactics as the Soviet Union might employ, to play them off against each other and to drive a wedge between them and the United States. But the lack of unity will be hurtful in their dealings with the United States as well, especially in issues in which America and its European allies, on the whole, will not be in agreement. And the number as well as the gravity of such issues will not diminish. U.S.-West European relations are likely to be dominated for the rest of this decade and into the 1990s by economic rivalry. Straitened economic circumstances under which all market economies operate will give rise to protectionist tendencies, which may find expression in the levying of discriminatory customs duties on each other's

products (steel, agricultural goods) and in monetary
policies designed to undercut each other. Substantially divergent--if not contradictory--perceptions of
the motivations underlying Soviet policy (domestic and
foreign) and the proper approaches the West should take
in dealing with the Soviet Union will exacerbate policy
differences about the terms on which East-West trade
should be conducted.[23] Opposing philosophies and
practices about North-South economic relations will be
a further source of discord. In general, the West will
be deprived of the advantage of coherent economic policies. West European countries are primarily trading
nations, and they may be more adversely affected by
world economic developments than the United States.
Although it has the largest dollar volume of foreign
trade of any country in the world, the United States
derives only about 8 percent of its GNP from exports in comparison with 25 percent for the EEC as a
whole.

Clearly, the repercussions of economic problems
will make themselves felt in the military realm.
European governments, by and large, will find it politically inexpedient to generate resources for military purposes to the detriment of social expenditures,
for fear of being voted out of office and contributing
to the destabilization of their country's political
structure. By attempting to fend off the destabilization of their political structures, they will increasingly irritate the American people and government.
They thus will help to undermine the stability of the
Western alliance, unless they meet with much more understanding in the United States than they have any
right to expect. The upshot of all this inevitably
will be a further deterioration of the military power
relationship between NATO and the Warsaw Pact in the
West's disfavor. This deterioration need not be so
precipitous as to render NATO defenseless. Barring
some sort of sudden move, such as the withdrawal of
U.S. troops or of U.S. nuclear weapons from Europe, or
the withdrawal of one or more key European countries
from NATO, the alliance should be capable of deterring
a Warsaw Pact attack and of defending itself if an attack occurs.

The real danger, in my view, rests in the serious
erosion of the political cohesiveness of the Western
alliance, as a result of misunderstandings among its
members which are not cleared up in timely fashion
and/or irreconcilable differences in their assessment
of policies that should be adopted in dealing with the
Soviet Union. Questions pertaining to military pre-
paredness form only a part of the problem. At issue is
the totality of the relationship between West and East,
of which the military is one aspect, albeit a very
important one.

As far as the military is concerned, perhaps literally no one in Western Europe has any illusion that a credible defense against the Warsaw Pact is possible without the United States. And there are, at least statistically (on the basis of public opinion surveys in several countries), relatively few people who would entrust their future to the tender mercies of the Soviet Union. The need for NATO is not questioned. Only fringe groups advocate withdrawal from the organization or its unilateral dissolution. But a growing number of people are developing doubts and fears about the military proclivities of the United States. Some are afraid that the United States cannot be relied on for protection; others (and there are increasing numbers of these) are concerned that the United States is only too willing to conduct a war limited to Europe. The bottom line is that West Europeans generally-- although not uniformly--are excessively dependent on the United States. In a period of renewed international tensions, which they tend to attribute to the truculence of the present American administration rather than the recalcitrance of the Soviet Union, they give vent to their helplessness by turning against the United States, without which their future security is not guaranteed and with which their future survival might be jeopardized.

Europeans find themselves confronting a dilemma from which they cannot easily escape. Their political attitudes reflect a general aversion to war, which is strengthened by a mind-boggling anxiety over the destructiveness of nuclear weapons. Opposition to nuclear weapons is expressed in a variety of agitational forms, which do nothing to enhance harmony between the European members of NATO and the United States.

Other considerations also need to be taken into account. Under the impact of the practical experiences of the past decade or so, many Europeans acquired an image of the Soviet Union that is substantially at variance with that which currently prevails in the United States. During this decade, processes of interaction among European states received considerable attention and showed some promising signs of possible development in the direction of a mutually tolerable framework of peaceful cooperation between essentially incompatible social systems. Despite the obvious and growing military might of the Soviet Union, that country somehow lost something of its menacing mystique for Europeans. Not that many Europeans believe in the peaceful intentions of the Soviet Union, but a large number of them do not think that the Soviet Union--like Hitler--is bent on reckless military aggression. On the contrary, they consider Soviet leaders as cautious, conservative, calculating, and persevering in their endeavors, and that they appear quite manageable.

The economic and social backwardness of the Soviet Union has also been glaringly exposed, as have the weaknesses of the Soviet-built empire in Eastern Europe. Europeans tend to take heart from these observations. Unlike many Americans, they tend to feel that terms of cooperation between West and East can be consolidated and that it is desirable to try to do so, difficult as it is to coexist with the Soviet Union.

The geographic imperatives really allow for no alternative. The Soviet Union is a neighbor. Ignoring it or trying to exclude it from European political and economic processes is futile. One way or another, the Soviet Union will assert itself in European affairs-- the question is only how. A confrontational relationship holds out no prospect whatever. Despite its socio-economic backwardness and the weaknesses of its empire, the Soviet Union cannot be forced to its knees economically and defeated militarily.

Punishment is an inappropriate concept in international relations and sanctions have a notorious record of failure, even in their application against lesser powers. Western Europe and America will be at odds with each other, to the detriment of both, if the United States will concentrate on isolating the Soviet Union and forcing it through external pressures to admit past wrongdoings, to pledge adherence to the rules of the game as defined by the West, and, in the final analysis, to undergo essential change. To avoid working at cross-purposes, the transatlantic allies will have to regulate their relations anew and put them on a more solid footing.

In my view, a reconciliation of the differences now plaguing the Western alliance will not be easily achieved. On the contrary, the fissures that have opened up in the alliance will grow wider and deeper. The United States and its European allies will drift further apart, and it is in this condition of disarray that West European countries will have to cope with the Soviet Union and Eastern Europe.

IV

For their part, the Soviet Union and the East European countries will be more difficult to deal with in the 1980s than they have been, especially in the first half of the 1970s. Any expectation of spectacular progress in working out terms for closer cooperation is bound to be disappointed. A climate of good feeling which coincided with rapidly expanding trade relations and somewhat eased political relations (marked by confidence-building efforts) has long since waned. It has given way to an atmosphere of wary exploration characterized by a slow, halting pace of mutual interactions.

The limits of a possible relaxation of tensions were rather quickly reached and could not be transcended easily. For the Soviet Union, the 1970s were not a decade of unmitigated success in its European policies. Achievements were at least partially offset--if not in fact nullified--by failures. Not even the Helsinki agreement, which the Soviet Union regarded as the pinnacle of success of its policy of detente, turned out to be a very serviceable vehicle for forging a new European order, Soviet-style. Instead, the Helsinki agreement was seized upon by the United States as an instrument with which to browbeat the Communist systems for their persistent violations of the human rights provisions contained in "basket three."

In the political arena, the Soviet Union was able to improve its image and favorably influence various segments of European publics concerning the existence of a community of interest on. the continent in the promotion of peace. (Not even Afghanistan had a lasting detrimental influence on this image.) In the ideological realm, the Soviet Union made scant headway, if any. More likely it suffered reverses, for the period of detente coincided with the expansion of Eurocommunism and the extraordinary erosion of the ideological bonds holding the socialist countries together. If anything, these were susceptible to ideological penetration and had to combat a variety of forms of "dissidence."

In the economic sphere, the Soviet Union was intensely disappointed at the resistance to vastly expanded relations which it encountered in the United States. Significant improvements in economic relations with Western European countries helped to mitigate the setback suffered at the hand of the United States Senate. But the management of the foreign economic policies of the socialist states left a great deal to be desired. Most of them overextended themselves in their borrowing from Western sources, and one (Poland) made the fatal error of restructuring its economy to fit a production pattern geared excessively to the import of products from Western industrial countries and to the sale of goods to developing countries. The Soviet Union itself avoided the worst pitfalls of imprudent management of its foreign economic policy. It began retrenching on foreign loans at a relatively early stage in order not to incur a huge balance of payments deficit.[24] It also curtailed imports of certain products from suppliers with whom it had an unfavorable trade balance. But it either failed to alert its East European allies to the trouble for which they were heading, or it did not succeed in persuading them to mend their ways. As a result, the Soviet Union has had to suffer the consequences of irresponsible management on the part of its allies. Economic integration among socialist countries has all but broken down. Still worse, all of the socialist economies--including the Soviet--have given incontrovertible evidence of fundamental systemic flaws that will prove extremely difficult to correct without impairing the integrity of the entire control system on which the Communist parties base their domination.

In military matters, the Soviet Union has succeeded in maintaining a numerical superiority of forces in Europe and in modernizing its array of armaments that further enhance its position vis-a-vis NATO. At the same time, the Soviet Union has been unsuccessful in negotiating arms control agreements that would be advantageous to it. Currently it faces the prospect of a new threat to its security in the form of American intermediate-range nuclear missiles deployed in Europe, within easy reach of Soviet territory, and it also must contend with a possible impairment of the Warsaw Pact structure as a result of ongoing Polish developments.

The crisis of Communism in Poland, which the Soviet Union has so far found more prudent not to handle in the manner in which it disposed of rebellions in East Germany, Hungary, and Czechoslovakia, is by all odds the outstanding failure Moscow has had to endure in its efforts to secure Eastern Europe as a reliable operational base and buffer against the West. Regardless of what happens in Poland proper, the inescapable conclusion one has to reach is that the mighty Soviet Union in thirty-five years has failed miserably in subjugating and dominating an essentially hapless and weak group of smallish countries on its borders.

Under these circumstances and in the face of palpable American hostility, the Soviet Union is not likely to be inclined toward bold new ventures in Europe. The prospect of further expansion of economic relations is dim, at least until the debts of East European countries have been brought under control and, perhaps, until the socialist systems have become more competitive in the international arena by having overcome their most glaring structural problems. These structural problems, however, will be far more difficult to cope with in the absence of massive infusions of Western investment capital and technology. The Soviet Union will struggle to secure an adequate hard currency supply for itself by judicious manipulation of exports of energy and raw materials to West European customers. But on the whole, seen in the broader context of overall trade volumes (on the part of the Soviet Union and its West European trading partners), these will be relatively insignificant initiatives. They will certainly not suffice to alleviate the basic economic problems that beset the Soviet Union.

The foreign economic policies of the Soviet Union, therefore, will not constitute a major threat to the

economies of Western Europe. By the same token, Eastern markets will not hold out a promise of relief for
hard-pressed Western exporting countries.

Poland will constitute a special problem for some
time. It remains to be seen if and on what terms the
Soviet Union would be willing to countenance a major
international rescue operation designed to bail out the
Polish economy, provided that such an operation would
materialize. At best, with everyone cooperating (including the Polish workers), such an unprecedented
operation could help to alleviate East-West tensions
and to lead to greater cooperation in other areas. At
worst, such an operation could be a disaster for all
who are associated with it. The risks involved are
enormous, and it is questionable if Western banks would
be ready to provide the needed capital, even under
government prodding and guarantees.

In the military realm, the Soviet Union is likely
to maintain mounting pressure on Western Europe by virtue of a relentless improvement of its military capability. At the same time, it is unlikely that the
Soviet Union will escalate its military pressures to
the point of their constituting an acute threat of war.
Under such circumstances, the members of NATO would
have no option but to close ranks with the United
States in a joint defense effort. From the Soviet
point of view this would be a highly undesirable development. Nurturing divisive trends in NATO is a far
more promising gambit which can be pursued at low risk
by political means. To show its good will, the Soviet
Union might be amenable to a negotiated troop reduction
scheme in the context of the Vienna MBFR talks. Agreement in the INF talks in Geneva appears far off in the
distant future, unless the position of the United
States changes drastically and both France and Great
Britain agree to have their nuclear forces drawn into
the negotiations. As matters now stand, the Soviet
Union has little to lose from dragging out these talks
indefinitely.

In the political realm, there appears to be relatively little room for maneuver on a government-to-
government basis. The Soviet Union is likely to proceed
with caution, although it will steadfastly seek to
exploit any opening provided by discord in the Western
alliance. Similarly, it will not relent in its propaganda campaign aimed at promoting anti-American, anti-
nuclear sentiment. It will foster by all means at its
disposal European peace movements, through which it
will seek to undermine the will of West European populations to support military programs commensurate with
the needs of an adequate defense. The success of these
efforts, of course, will be predicated on the deftness
with which the Soviet Union conducts the campaign to
which it obviously attributes great importance. But in

large measure,   the success of Soviet efforts will also
depend on how credible the charges raised against the
United States will be and how adroitly the United
States manages to counter the Soviet campaign.
     Among various European countries, the Federal
Republic of Germany will remain by far the most likely
target on which Soviet foreign policy will concentrate,
just as it has been since the late 1960s.   This is not
because the Soviet Union necessarily harbors fond feelings for the West Germans; the contrary may be true.
But West Germany occupies a central place in the defense of Western Europe, and in other respects, too, it
plays a very significant part in the Western alliance.
At the same time, the Federal Republic is peculiarly
susceptible to Soviet manipulation because of a number
of   peculiar conditions that affect its existence.   It
is therefore a prize worth "capturing," for the Soviet
Union would be much closer to a hegemonial position in
Europe if it succeeded in loosening the ties between
West Germany and other Western countries (perhaps especially the United States).   Still better, it aspires to
wean the Federal Republic of Germany away from the
alliance system in which it has been embedded since the
1950s.

V

     The "special situation" of the Federal Republic of
Germany was described with rare candor by Chancellor
Helmut Schmidt in an interview with the Hamburg weekly
Die Zeit on April 16, 1982.   According to the chancel-
lor:

          The Federal Republic of Germany and the
     Germans living here find themselves in a
     categorically different situation from that
     of the French and the English.
          First of all, the Federal Republic of
     Germany borders on that part of Europe in
     which the presence of broadly and strongly
     deployed Soviet military power infringes upon
     our sense of security.
          Secondly, in contrast to France and
     England, the Federal Republic of Germany does
     not have its own nuclear weapons, does not
     want to have them, and should not have them.
     As such, it is completely dependent in the
     nuclear field on the willingness of the
     United States of America to lend us its nu-
     clear umbrella and protection.
          Thirdly, in the conceivable case of a
     conventional war, the some 240,000-odd square
     kilometers the Federal Republic of Germany
     consists of will be both the initial and the

central battlefield, not French territory and
by no means English territory.

Fourthly, deep inside us there is the
highly significant awareness of the division
of our nation, the knowledge not only that it
would inevitably be the Germans who would
have to suffer most on both sides of the
present dividing line, but also that even in
peace every aggravation, every additional bit
of tension, can result in making connections
between the Germans here and there even worse
than they are today. We know that they are
much better today than they were twenty years
ago at the time of the Khrushchev ultimatum
or the building of the Berlin Wall. This
improvement may be only slight, but it is
very important for us Germans and we wish to
leave it as intact as possible.

Fifthly, there's the awareness of Berlin's geo-strategic insular situation.

Sixthly, we should add to this the willingness of our people, in view of all these
special factors, to entrust their freedom
from foreign pressures or orders to the protection of the United States of America and
the protection provided by our other allies.
The extent to which this willingness is present in the German people was expressed by a
Gallup poll recently taken in all of Europe,
in which it was shown that Germans, much more
than Italians, French, or English, pin their
hopes on American protection and are willing
to accept the presence of American nuclear
weapons on their own soil for this purpose.

Candid as the chancellor was, he might well have
elaborated further on some of the points he made. He
may have listed other special conditions which differ-
entiate the "Germans living in the Federal Republic"
from other European nations, not just France and Eng-
land.

One such condition is an exceptionally weak sense
of national identity and a low level of self-
esteem.[25] The West Germans chafe under the trunca-
tion of "their" country. While they sincerely profess
not to seek a reunification with East Germany as a
practical goal that would be realizable in the near
future, they have a longing for national unity with the
East German population. This longing appears to be
growing stronger rather than weaker with the passage of
time, and it may well become the source of a romantic
nationalism in the future (under conditions of adversity and frustration with the Western allies) that
would lead increasing numbers of West Germans to seek

fulfillment of their national destiny in some sort of compromise with the East. For it is clear that any rapprochement with the Germans living in the German Democratic Republic can only take place with the con-sent--if not at the behest--of the Soviet Union.

This is not to say that a new Rapallo or something akin to the Stalin-Hitler pact is in the offing. Both the Federal Republic of Germany and the Soviet Union are far from the right psychological moment for such a spectacular move. But it is obvious that through the German Democratic Republic the Soviet Union is able to exert--and is certainly straining to exert--pressures on the Federal Republic that would make the Bonn gov-ernment more amenable to "reasonableness" in European affairs (at the moment, up to and including the rejec-tion of deployment of American intermediate-range nu-clear missiles on the territory of the Federal Repub-lic).

The German Democratic Republic is both the carrot and stick with which the Federal Republic is enticed or threatened, as the case may be. And Berlin is the Achilles heel of the Federal Republic of Germany. Thus far, the responses of the Federal Republic have given no cause for alarm. Bonn has not permitted itself to be blackmailed and it has made no concessions of major consequence. But the relationship between the two German states in no way corresponds to their relative power positions. East Germany, which is far weaker in almost every respect and which has had monumental dif-ficulties in the past in preventing its population from fleeing en masse to the West, has the whip hand even in regard to a sense of national identity. Ever more assertively it is East Germany that claims to be the legatee of the Prussian past, of the glory of the German empire. It is there that the roots of German language and the cradle of German culture may be found. Similarly, it is East Germany, which badly needs West German economic assistance, that sets the terms--and harsh terms they are--of the specific forms of inter-relationship between the two states. West Germany permanently finds itself in the role of the suitor seeking favors, regardless of how often it is rebuffed and what indignities are inflicted on it. The economic support West Germany provides to the German Democratic Republic amounts to several billion Deutsche Mark per year.[26] West German spokesmen emphasize the special responsibilities of the two German states in preserving calm and promoting friendly relations that would have a beneficial impact on the strained East-West relation-ship. Not too long ago, the same spokesmen insisted that an improvement in these relations would be contin-gent on an improved East-West climate.

There is no question but that a special relation-ship exists between the two German states and that, in

the normal course of events, the two states will draw
closer together. The crucial question is on whose
terms the rapprochement will proceed, and what impact
it will ultimately have on power alignments in Europe.
There are other special conditions as well, which
are worth recording.

Because of its geographic location, if for no
other reason, the Federal Republic of Germany is more
fearful of the consequences of military hostilities in
Europe than are other countries which are essentially
shielded by West Germany. Should there be another war
in Europe, the Federal Republic of Germany (or at any
rate a significant portion of it) is certain to be
substantially destroyed, regardless of the outcome of
the war. The Federal Republic is thus in a somewhat
schizophrenic frame of mind concerning military power
and its uses. On the one hand, it is deeply interested
in a strong defense including a powerful nuclear component; on the other hand, it is profoundly desirous of
avoiding war. It exalts deterrence and abhors the
prospect of war fighting.

Because of this special condition, the peace movement has taken hold more strongly than in some other
Western countries. It has been able to capitalize on
widespread and deep anguish, not just among the young
but among broad strata of the population.

The large number of foreign troops stationed in
West Germany are also a source of friction with the
German population. While the troops are there to provide protection against a potential aggressor from the
East, their presence is somehow reminiscent of Germany's defeat in the last war. An increasing number of
people, especially the young who are dismally ignorant
of the recent past, have a feeling that the occupation
regime which followed Germany's unconditional surrender
has never been terminated. They feel that foreign
troops, especially Americans who are present in the
largest numbers, encroach on the sovereignty of the
Federal Republic and interfere with the "normal" development of the country. Irritation at being a place
d'armes teeming with foreign troops and bristling with
foreign arms to date has not played a significant role
in shaping German popular opinion, but it is a special
feature of the realities of existence in West Germany
which could have an adverse influence on harmonious
alliance relations.

Because of its historic legacy, the Federal Republic of Germany is experiencing somewhat greater difficulties than other European countries with its own
youth, which have simply not been subjected to adequate
socialization. They have not been sufficiently in-
structed about the Hitler period and the immediate
aftermath of the war (U.S. economic assistance, and so
forth), so that they are not able to appreciate either

the American contribution to their country's recovery
or the positive values and achievements of the system
under which they live. Unlike their elders, they do
not stand in awe of the United States for its unmatched
power and democratic achievements. Instead, they see a
much more tarnished America, defeated in Vietnam, prone
to imperialist intervention in Central America and
elsewhere, suffering from widespread economic misery
and political turmoil (witness the frequent changes in
political leadership). In the current situation of
stress, they tend to see mainly the negative aspects of
their country's social, economic, and political order.
Hence, they are more apt to be critical and rebellious
and are searching for an alternative to the system,
instead of being satisfied with modifying it.[27]

To be sure, not all and perhaps not even a majority of the young people are in this frame of mind.
But it is a characteristic trait of the Germans, at
least in the present period, to overstate the challenges presented by the young (who in the past have
generally been docile). Members of the older generation, especially those active in the political life of
the country, feel an exaggerated sense of responsibility to deal with the problem, without having a very
clear notion of how they should cope with it. Co-
opting the young into the established political parties
is not the answer. In order to preserve their integrity and their independence, the young are inclined to
form their own organizations, which in the German setting inevitably take on a political coloration and make
their presence felt in the political arena. The party
system and distribution of power in elected governing
bodies is affected by this development, and the foundations of parliamentary democracy are endangered.

Because of the demographic development of the Federal Republic of Germany, its armed forces face a
serious shortage of recruits beginning in the mid-
1980s. So far, no acceptable solution for this problem
has been found, although the Ministry of Defense has
commissioned a report on the long-range needs of the
military.[28] The recruitment of women to replace men
in certain non-combat functions--though considered by
some as a possible option--has met with widespread
opposition. Unless answers are found, the Bundeswehr
will shrink by nearly 50 percent in the course of the
coming ten years.

A problem of entirely different character confronts the Federal Republic in the form of a sizable
and rapidly expanding foreign population, whose growth
is due both to natural increase and migration. This
stands in sharp contrast with a decline in the German
population, due to an exceedingly low rate of reproduction and a relatively high rate of mortality among
elder people.[29] The number of foreigners now exceeds

4.5 million (7.2 percent of the population). For 1990, it is estimated that their ranks will swell to 7 million, or 12.5 percent of the total population of the country, unless drastic measures are taken to curtail the influx of new settlers and to encourage the departure of those who have no jobs. The German authorities up to now have desisted from adopting stringent measures because of their sense of guilt about the treatment of foreign workers by the Hitlerite regime.

The Federal Republic of Germany, of course, does not face a unique problem. Percentage-wise, Switzerland has many more foreigners (13.9 percent), and in absolute numbers, France with 4.1 million is a close second to the Federal Republic. There are also 2 million foreigners in Great Britain. Nor has the Federal Republic witnessed riots akin to those that rocked Great Britain in the early 1980s. Yet there are grounds for concern about the ability of the German people and of their authorities to handle the social and political problems that will arise from so many foreigners living in their midst. These problems already exist, especially in regard to Turks who now form the largest single group of foreigners and who pose greater problems than others because of their reluctance to assimilate.[30] Unemployment among foreigners is twice as high as among the native population. What this means is that the government pays out huge sums to foreigners in unemployment compensation (at the current rate, DM 3 billion per year), for child support (at the current rate, DM 2.5 billion per year), and other social assistance. Because of substantially different rates of reproduction, German schools are being overrun by the children of foreigners. In Munich, 25 percent of the children now entering elementary school are foreigners, while in Frankfurt the percentage is expected to reach 70 by the beginning of the 1990s.[31]

Signs of mounting discontent among the Germans are evident, and instances of brutal violence (including murder) against foreigners, especially Turks, are reported with increasing frequency.[32] In some quarters, it is an open secret that the Turks of the present and future are viewed as the Jews of yesterday.

Due to the structure of the West German economy, foreign trade impacts heavily on people's lives in the Federal Republic of Germany. Exports account for one-quarter of the GNP, and one in every four jobs is dependent on foreign trade. For this reason and because of unusually bad memories connected with the economic crises in the 1920s and early 1930s, West Germans react with much greater concern than do other European nations to any signs of a downturn in their economy. The oil shocks of the 1970s impelled them to seek secure supplies of energy and raw materials, to protect themselves as much as possible from the

vagaries of the oil markets.[33]   This is a major reason for their interest in the gas pipe line deal   with
the Soviet Union.   Their general interest in trade with
Eastern Europe,   however,   has historic roots.   Traditionally,   a   substantial   portion of their   trade   was
conducted in the Central and East European region.   In
the inter-war period, they dominated this area economically.   They thus reacted with alacrity when opportunities   for   expanded economic   relations   opened   up
again   in   the   1970s.   West German   banks   lent   more
heavily--and   perhaps on less stringent terms--to Eastern   borrowers than did other   financial   institutions,
and the volume of trade between the Federal Republic of
Germany and the Soviet Union,   in particular, grew rapidly.
     The Federal Republic is the Soviet Union's largest
Western trading partner.   Trade between the two   countries   grew elevenfold   between 1970 and 1981,   when it
amounted to nearly DM 17 billion.   But this is exactly
2.2 percent   of the   Federal Republic's total   foreign
trade   volume   in 1981.   While trade with   the   Federal
Republic represents over 5 percent of the total foreign
trade   of the Soviet Union,   it is   lower by 45 percent
than   Soviet trade with the German Democratic Republic,
nearly   25 percent less than Soviet trade with   Czechoslovakia,   Poland,   and   Bulgaria,   and almost   exactly
equal to Soviet trade with Hungary.
     As for the trade patterns of the Federal   Republic
of   Germany,   nearly 45 percent of its imports and   exports are accounted for by France,   Italy,   Great Britain,   and   the Benelux countries (with the   Netherlands
being   the largest supplier of the Federal Republic and
France   its   top customer).[34] The entire   volume   of
West   German   trade with the Soviet Union   and   Eastern
Europe (excluding the German Democratic   Republic)   is
less   (4.5 percent in 1981) than the trade volume   with
Switzerland.   This figure, however, should be augmented
by the amount of trade with East Germany (1.3 percent),
which West Germans insistently refer to under the separate heading of "inner-German trade."
     While   it   appears   that the Federal   Republic   of
Germany trades more heavily with the East than do other
West European countries, in point of fact, the percentage of the foreign trade of several of these   countries
with the East is not appreciably lower (Italy, 4.4 percent;   Switzerland,   4.2 percent;   France, 4.1 percent;
and   Sweden,   3.7 percent).   By comparison, the   East
accounts for 11.7 percent of Austria's foreign   trade,
but only 2.5 percent of that of Great Britain.[35]
     It   is   not sufficient to rely on   raw,   undiffer-
entiated   percentages of trade as a reliable   indicator
of   the   importance of economic relations among   countries.   On the whole, however, it would appear that the
Federal   Republic is not excessively dependent   on   nor

vulnerable to its trade relations with the East. If all business with the Communist countries of Eastern Europe were to cease overnight, only about one German worker in a hundred would lose his job. By the same token, the Federal Republic has become too closely integrated into the European Economic Community (to which it is the major contributor) to be easily detachable from its association with the EEC, even under adverse conditions affecting the economies of all West European industrial societies.

The dangers the West German economy faces lurk elsewhere, notably in a generally shrinking world market and a restructuring of trade patterns in the world economy. Such developments would cause profound dislocations in the West German economy. Under such circumstances, there may be a temptation on the part of some to look for new markets among the Communist countries of Eastern Europe. But these will hardly be in a position to absorb a larger share of West German products and will not be able to offer the Federal Republic relief from its economic calamities, nor to exploit these calamities to their advantage.

In the absence of other remedies, West German business interests are casting about for expanded markets in the Third World. Their search in this direction is based on dubious expectations, for the developing countries themselves are suffering from almost insurmountable economic problems. Different solutions may have to be found to revitalize the German economy, which has been a mainstay of the country's stability, having brought full employment and prosperity to the population as a whole.

The 1980s shape up as a period of unprecedented difficulties for the Federal Republic of Germany, both in foreign and domestic affairs. The stability that has been the hallmark of this successor state of the Third Reich will be tested by a variety of unsettling trends in alliance relations, matters of security policy, and relations with the Eastern countries.

As the country enters these trying years, it will also experience a change of government, reflecting a realignment of power among the traditional post-war parties. The social-liberal coalition (SPD-FDP) which has governed since the late 1960s has lost the support of the majority of the electorate and is approaching a parting of the ways between its constituent members. It is possible that by the time this report is printed a new governing coalition composed of the conservative parties (CDU-CSU) and the FDP (whose adherence the conservatives desire, in order to assure themselves of a solid majority) will be in office.[36] At the latest, a shift in power will take place following the parliamentary elections scheduled for the fall of 1984.[37]

This shift will not bring about significant changes in the substance of either foreign or domestic policies, although the style and the rhetoric (which are not without importance) will certainly be different. With luck, the conservative-liberal coalition (provided that the liberals survive at the polls, which is not certain)[38] or an outright conservative government will still be in office at the turn of the decade. But it will have to rule in a country rent by social and political unrest. There is no doubt that police power will have to be invoked to a far greater degree than in the years since World War II. This will rekindle fears in the country and abroad about the resurgence of German authoritarianism.

Meanwhile, the political spectrum, which thus far has excluded a far right and far left, will be broadened. Under the impact of its political failures, the SPD will probably come under the sway of its more ideologically oriented and more militant wing, which is strongly opposed to nuclear armament and tends to be less critical of the Soviet Union than the current SPD-led government of Helmut Schmidt. The party will probably not attract more than 25 or 30 percent of the electorate, or perhaps even less.[39]

In addition to a radicalized SPD, another grouping is also certain to become a permanent fixture on the political scene. The so-called Greens and the Alternative List--separately or jointly, as the case may be-- have already made their mark in several state elections (notably Berlin and Hamburg) and will unquestionably poll a sufficient number of votes (a minimum of 5 percent is required by law) to enter the Bundestag for the first time in 1984.[40]

Supported preponderantly by young people, the Greens and the Alternative List (often referred to under the initials GAL) are more a political movement than a party in the traditional cast. They are not communists in the accepted sense of that designation, although some of their members are former or current members of the minuscule German Communist party (DKP), and they are obviously targeted for penetration by the Soviet Union through the East German Communist party (SED). They harbor among their members individuals with leanings toward fascism and many who could most aptly be called populists. The GAL is not homogeneous. It is more an agglomeration of various groups, including environmentalists and pacifists. Many of their members now reject cooperation with any established political party; and while they do not refuse to serve in elected assemblies, they fundamentally oppose standard parliamentary procedures.

The GAL, of course, are strongly against nuclear armament and are thus closely connected with the peace movement. There is also a pronounced anti-American bias in their policy proclamations. While they pay lip service to the necessity of reciprocal disarmament between opposing power blocs in Europe and profess that they do not favor the unilateral dissolution of NATO, their line of argumentation is frequently indistinguishable from that promulgated by the Soviet Union.

The presence of the GAL in the political life of the Federal Republic will introduce an element of strife into politics which the country has not known before. Should the SPD and the GAL join in causes they both support--and that is likely, as in regard to nuclear armament--they will present a formidable challenge to the conservative government. The question really will be how certain policies can be implemented in the face of a vocal and militant opposition, representing as much as 35 to 40 percent of the electorate. No one can be certain of the outcome, although the danger is not very acute that the democratic structure of the country will suffer irreparable danger and that the government will be so paralyzed as to be unable to maintain law and order.

In the long run, further changes in the political spectrum of the country may be anticipated. From discontented elements (perhaps in all parties), a new left-of-center, liberal-socialist grouping, somewhat akin to the Social Democratic party of Great Britain, may emerge. This party could have very broad appeal to the electorate, and in due time it could win sufficient support to assume leadership of the government.

VI

While the anticipated evolution of the Federal Republic of Germany contains unique features, it will not be fundamentally different from that of other West European countries. The viability of the advanced industrial democracies individually and in alliance with each other will be sorely tested, but so will be the viability of the socialist systems in the East.

The competition between the two systems, though it will not be devoid of cooperative features serving the interests of both sides, will be more acute and more confrontational than it was in the 1970s. The military power of the Soviet Union will pervade all relations between East and West, but it will not be decisive in establishing the hegemony of the Soviet Union over Europe. It is difficult to imagine that the Soviet Union would not play a significant role in European affairs. Any degree of Soviet dominance, however, will be determined less by the military power of the Soviet Union than by the ability of the Western powers in concert with the United States to combine their assets in an effort to preserve the basic values as well as the institutional underpinnings of their democratic

systems. The prospects for the West at this writing
are not too bright. Prudence would counsel a pessimis-
tic prognosis, but it is nowhere foreordained that the
Western countries cannot remain masters of their own
destiny.

NOTES

1. Hans Rühle, "The Theater Nuclear Issue in
German Politics," Strategic Review (Spring 1981): 54-
60. The author was appointed chief of the minister's
Planning Staff in the Ministry of Defense of the Kohl
government in October 1982.
2. Manfred Wörner, "The 'Peace Movement' and NATO:
An Alternative View from Bonn," Strategic Review (Winter 1982): 15-21. The author was appointed minister
of defense in the Kohl government in October 1982.
3. Colonel Mozes W.A. Weers (Ret.), "The Nuclear
Debate in the Netherlands," Strategic Review (Spring
1981): 67-77.
4. Wörner, "The 'Peace Movement' and NATO," 16.
5. Following the breakup of the government coalition in October 1982, the Social Democratic party
gradually veered away from the course steered by Helmut
Schmidt and adopted an increasingly negative attitude
toward missile deployment.
6. See Frans A.M. Alting von Geusau, "Die Nieder-
lande und die Modernisierung der Kernwaffen," Europa-
Archiv (January 25, 1982): 29-38.
7. Brezhnev's successor, Yuri V. Andropov, has
continued this practice. If anything, Andropov has
spoken about the military confrontation in Europe with
greater frequency and openness than his predecessor and
has expounded familiar Soviet themes more vigorously.
8. An outstanding example of this sort of activity
is a publication called Whence the Threat to Europe.
It was issued in 1981 under the aegis of the Soviet
Committee for European Security and Cooperation and
represents the collective effort of a group of authors
referred to as the Scientific Research Council on Peace
and Disarmament. Published by Progress Publishers in
Moscow and translated into several languages, this
87-page paperback pamphlet was widely distributed free
of charge. It addresses a multitude of problems relat-
ing to the military confrontation in Europe with remarkable frankness, in easily comprehensible question-
and-answer form. In 1983 a second, improved and updated version of this pamphlet appeared under the title
How to Avert the Threat to Europe.
9. This practice has continued under the leadership of Yuri V. Andropov. Among the most frequently
available high-level spokesmen are Vadim V. Zagladin,
first deputy chief of the party's International

Department, Valentin M. Falin, an editorial commentator for _Izvestia_ (transferred to that post from the party's International Information Department), Aleksander Bovin, also an editorial commentator for _Izvestia_, and Colonel General Nikolai F. Chervov, an arms control expert on the General Staff of the Soviet Armed Forces.

   10. For a text of the Krefeld Appeal and related materials, see _Ist der Nukleare Rüstungswettlauf Unvermeidbar?_, Dokumente herausgegeben von Klaus Hübotter (Fürth, 1981).

   11. _Time_, October 19, 1981, 52.

   12. See Christopher Jon Lamb, "Public Opinion and Nuclear Weapons in Europe: A Report on the Twenty-seventh Session of the North Atlantic Assembly," _NATO Review_ (December 1981): 30.

   13. Jürgen Leinemann, "Die Angst der Deutschen," _Spiegel-Buch_ (Hamburg: Rowohlt, February 1982), 161. By way of comparison with the German figures, a recent poll conducted in Great Britain revealed that 53 percent of those questioned opposed LRTNF deployment in Western Europe, while in Holland in February 1981, 30 percent favored deployment on Dutch territory and 54 percent supported the removal of _all_ nuclear weapons from the country.

In summer 1983, it was alleged that in the Federal Republic of Germany 75 percent of the population opposed the deployment of Pershing IIs and GLCMs. Actual results of a poll publicized on West German television in late August indicated that in the event the United States and the USSR did not reach agreement in the Geneva INF talks, 14 percent would favor deployment, while 22 percent opposed it and 50 percent would prefer the continuation of negotiations. Nearly half of those questioned (47 percent) were of the opinion that American missiles would represent a threat to the Federal Republic, 25 percent thought that the missiles would contribute to greater security, and 28 percent professed to have no opinion.

   14. See, for example, a stinging condemnation of the laxity of Europeans to do enough in their own behalf in Justin Galen, "An Open Letter to NATO Leaders: Theater Nuclear Weapons and the Crisis in Europe's Leadership," _Armed Forces JOURNAL International_ (November 1981): 42-48.

   15. As Walter Laqueur noted in a recent survey of European political attitudes, "In Europe no one expects an attack on the central front." See Walter Laqueur, "Euro-Neutralism," _Commentary_ (June 1980): 23.

   16. Jeffrey Record and Robert J. Hanks, _U.S. Strategy at the Crossroads_, Institute of Foreign Policy Analysis, as cited in the _International Herald Tribune_, July 12, 1982.

   17. Walter Laqueur, "Hollanditis: A New Stage in European Neutralism," _Commentary_ (August 1981): 19-26.

18. A Conference on Disarmament in Europe (CDE) is scheduled to open in Stockholm on January 17, 1984.

19. Frankfurter Allgemeine Zeitung, August 25, 1982.

20. Neue Zürcher Zeitung, August 12, 1982.

21. Figures for Denmark from Frankfurter Allgemeine Zeitung, August 13, 1982, and for Belgium from Tagesspiegel, August 15, 1982.

22. The flight of capital from France in a little over a year following the election of François Mitterand as president was reported to have reached catastrophic proportions. About 33 billion francs were said to have been illegally shipped out of the country. See Frankfurter Allgemeine Zeitung, July 31, 1982 and Tagesspiegel, August 20, 1982.

23. A major crisis in U.S.-West European relations was precipitated by President Reagan's decision on June 22, 1982, to invoke sanctions against European manufacturers in order to block the manufacture of U.S.-designed pipeline equipment (under license) destined for delivery to the Soviet Union. The West European reaction was sharply critical of U.S. trade and economic policies. The United States was accused of intruding on the sovereignty of its allies.

The absence of an agreed strategy for East-West economic relations is a serious threat to the coherence of the alliance. In addition to the controversy over the Siberian gas pipeline project, contentious issues include U.S. grain sales to the USSR, credits to Communist countries, the transfer of high technology, and economic pressure on the Soviet Union.

24. The hard currency debts of the CMEA (Council for Mutual Economic Assistance) countries--which include the Soviet Union, Bulgaria, Czechoslovakia, the German Democratic Republic, Hungary, Poland, and Romania--grew from a net of $31.2 billion in 1975 to $79 billion in 1981. With the exception of Bulgaria whose debt rose only modestly, the indebtedness of all other East European countries grew approximately three-fold in these six years. Poland stood out and constituted a special case largely because its debt in absolute figures was much higher than that of any other country: it grew from $7.7 billion in 1975 to $22 billion in 1981. By contrast, in the same period the indebtedness of the Soviet Union rose from $7.8 billion to $15.5 billion. It is perhaps worth noting that in 1975 the Soviet Union and Poland had hard currency debts of almost exactly the same magnitude, while in 1981, Soviet indebtedness was only two-thirds that of Poland.

Data from Dr. Thomas A. Layman, "Should Western Bank Credit to East European Nations be Suspended?", The International Economic and Financial Outlook (San Francisco: Crocker National Bank, Summer 1982).

25. For example, a cross-national study of public
attitudes in seven countries (the United States, Great
Britain, Japan, France, Italy, Spain, and the Federal
Republic of Germany) conducted by the West German
Allensbach Institute in spring 1982 revealed that only
21 percent of West Germans were "very proud" of their
nationality (the lowest percentage by far among all
seven countries), as compared with 80 percent in the
United States, 55 percent in Great Britain, 49 percent
in Spain, 41 percent in Italy, 33 percent in France,
and 30 percent in Japan. Extensive excerpts from this
study appear in Professor Elisabeth Noelle-Neumann
(head of Allensbach Institute), "Brauchen wir mehr
Nationalstolz?", Frankfurter Allgemeine Zeitung, August 6, 1982.

26. The Federal Republic of Germany does not release official figures on what may be called support
for the East German economy. This support is made up
of several components such as preferential terms of
trade (tariff concessions), revolving credits, contri-
butions to the building of transit roads through the
German Democratic Republic, various user fees for East
German transport and postal facilities, other types of
payments for services, compulsory currency exchanges
for visitors to the German Democratic Republic (at
parity rates between currencies, although the un-
official exchange rate between the Deutsche Mark and
the East German Mark is nearly one to five), monetary
and other gifts from West Germans to friends and relatives in the German Democratic Republic, and the average annual "purchase" of the freedom of 1,000 persons held in East German prisons, at a fixed rate of
DM 40,000 per head.

27. For a comprehensive study of German youth
attitudes, see Jugendwerk der deutschen Shell, Jugend
'81 (Opladen: Leske Verlag und Budrich GmbH, 1982).

28. Kommission für die Langzeitplanung der Bundeswehr, Bericht (Bonn, June 21, 1982).

29. According to a census taken on May 27, 1970,
the Federal Republic of Germany had a population of
60.65 million, including 2.98 million (4.9 percent)
foreigners. In 1981, the population of the Federal
Republic numbered 61.71 million, including 4.63 million
(7.5 percent) foreigners. Of 811,000 live births registered in the Federal Republic in 1970, foreigners
accounted for 63,000 (7.7 percent). The corresponding
figures for 1981 were 624,000 live births of which
80,000 (12.8 percent) were foreigners. Institut der
Deutschen Wirtschaft, Zahlen zur wirtschaftlichen
Entwicklung der Bundesrepublik Deutschland (Köln:
Deutscher Instituts Verlag GmbH, 1983), 1-2.

30. Turks are the most numerous national group
(1.546 million or 33 percent), followed next by Yugo-
slavs (637,000 or 15 percent) and Italians (624,000 or

14 percent). German Information Center, <u>Focus</u> <u>on</u> <u>Mi-</u>
<u>norities</u> <u>in</u> <u>Germany</u> (New York, July 1982).
    31. Lothar Julitz, "Dem europäischen Arbeitsmarkt
droht bis 1990 der Zusammenbruch," <u>Frankfurter</u> <u>Allge-</u>
<u>meine</u> <u>Zeitung</u>, July 9, 1982.
    32. On June 22, 1982, Chancellor Helmut Schmidt
convened a special meeting of political and community
leaders to discuss the "minorities problem." The chancellor expressed the view that "it is urgent for all
democratically inclinded groups to take action against
growing hostility toward foreigners," for if this development were permitted to continue, "then the face of
our [sic] country will change for the worse with consequences for domestic peace and for the way in which the
Federal Republic appears abroad." German Information
Center, <u>Focus</u> <u>on</u> <u>Minorities</u>.
    33. The Federal Republic's bill for crude oil
imports (exclusive of mineral oil products) increased
from DM 9.1 billion in 1973 to DM 44.7 billion in 1982.
Meanwhile, the quantity of oil imported decreased from
110.5 million tons in 1973 to 72.5 million tons in
1982. Institut der Deutschen Wirtschaft, <u>Zahlen</u> 1983,
71.
    In paying for their oil imports, the Federal Re-
public and other West European countries were also hard
hit by the unfavorable exchange rate that developed
between their currencies and the U.S. dollar in the
early 1980s, for oil purchases on the international
market are transacted in U.S. dollars. Between 1980
and 1982, the value of the Deutsche Mark as against the
dollar decreased by 33 percent.
    34. Lothar Julitz, Schatten auch über dem Export:
Eine Analyse des deutschen Aussenhandels, <u>Frankfurter</u>
<u>Allgemeine</u> <u>Zeitung</u>, August 30, 1982.
    The pattern of West German foreign trade is very
similar to that of the European Economic Community
(EEC) in general. The member countries of the EEC
conduct a little over 50 percent of their foreign trade
among themselves, an additional 12-13 percent with
other European OECD countries, approximately 7 percent
with the United States, less than 2 percent with Japan,
and under 5 percent with planned-economy countries.
    35. <u>Die</u> <u>Zeit</u>, June 11, 1982.
    36. On October 1, 1982, the social-liberal coali-
tion lost a "constructive" vote of no confidence in the
Bundestag, and on October 4, 1982, President Karl
Carstens entrusted Helmut Kohl, the leader of the
Christian Democratic Union, with the formation of a new
government. (A "constructive" vote of no confidence--
a vote in which another chancellor candidate is assured
of a majority--is the only means by which a government
can be toppled in the course of a parliamentary term.
This provision was written into the Constitution of the
Federal Republic of Germany to prevent a repetition of

the baneful experiences the Weimar Republic had with frequent changes in government.)

37. Because of the circumstances under which a change of government took place in October 1982, Chancellor Kohl called for new elections a year-and-a-half ahead of time, on March 6, 1983.

38. The Free Democratic party survived the parliamentary elections held on March 6, 1983, by polling 6.9 percent of the votes (as compared with 10.6 percent in 1980).

39. The Social Democratic party underwent a rapid radicalization during its first year as an opposition party. But it managed to retain most of its support in the parliamentary elections held on March 6, 1983, polling 38.2 percent of the votes (as compared with 42.9 percent in 1980).

40. The Greens polled 5.6 percent of the votes in the parliamentary elections held on March 6, 1983 (as compared with 1.5 percent in 1980), and placed 27 of their members in the newly elected Bundestag.